everyday

salads

Bath New York Singapore Hong Kong Cologne Delhi Melbourne

This edition published by Parragon in 2009

Parragon
Queen Street House
4 Queen Street
Bath
BA1 1HE, UK

Copyright © Parragon Books Ltd 2008
Cover design by Talking Design
Designed by Terry Jeavons & Company
Additional text written by Linda Doeser

ISBN 978-1-4075-5624-6

Printed in China

Notes for the Reader
This book uses both metric and imperial measurements. Follow the same units of measurement throughout; do not mix metric and imperial. All spoon measurements are level: teaspoons are assumed to be 5 ml, and tablespoons are assumed to be 15 ml. Unless otherwise stated, milk is assumed to be full fat, eggs and individual vegetables are medium, and pepper is freshly ground black pepper.

The times given are an approximate guide only. Preparation times differ according to the techniques used by different people and the cooking times may also vary from those given. Optional ingredients, variations or serving suggestions have not been included in the calculations.

Recipes using raw or very lightly cooked eggs should be avoided by infants, the elderly, pregnant women, convalescents and anyone suffering from an illness. Pregnant and breastfeeding women are advised to avoid eating peanuts and peanut products. Sufferers from nut allergies should be aware that some of the ready-made ingredients used in the

everyday
salads

introduction

Whether served as a summery main course, a refreshing side dish, an intriguing warm starter, an easy to transport picnic dish or a quick lunch, salads are wonderfully versatile. Ingredients ranging from meat, poultry, fish, cheese and eggs to vegetables, pulses, fruit, seeds, pasta and grains can be mixed and matched into endless delicious combinations. Dressings may be equally diverse – a squeeze of lemon and a drizzle of oil or a classic herb vinaigrette, creamy mayonnaise or a low-fat yogurt sauce, a combination of subtle Asian herbs and spices or a mind-blowing Caribbean concoction of tropical fruit juice and chillies.

Successful salads depend on using the best-quality ingredients. Limp leaves, over-ripe tomatoes, dried-up cheese and soggy pasta will not be improved by mixing them together or disguised by smothering them with dressing. Traditional salad ingredients, such as lettuce, cucumber

and celery, must be really fresh. Fruit, whether tomatoes and peppers or mangoes and strawberries, should be ripe and bursting with flavour. Keep an eye on the 'use-by' dates of storecupboard ingredients – nuts, seeds and oils quickly become rancid and ground spices soon lose their flavour. Finally, as a general rule, don't add the dressing to a salad until you are ready to serve it.

We are driven crazy these days with advice to eat more healthily and to include more fruit and vegetables in our diet. Salads make this easy as a mixture of different coloured fruit and vegetables – a typical salad – is guaranteed to provide a wide range of nutrients and plenty of fibre. Many ingredients are used raw thus conserving their vitamin content. Monounsaturated oils, such as

olive and rapeseed, help protect against high blood cholesterol, while the addition of seeds supplies essential omega-6. Finally, as flavourings for dressings – garlic, herbs, mustard, fruit juice, wine vinegars, nut oils – are so tasty, you'll find it easy to cut down your salt intake. Super foods with super flavour – on a plate.

classic salads

Many classic salads were first put together by family cooks mixing and matching the finest and freshest local ingredients into a harmonious combination and these quickly became regional specialities. Almost every country has its own favourite. What Italian could resist the partnership of melon and Parma ham and would a Greek consider a meal complete without a salad featuring juicy black olives, sun-ripened tomatoes and piquant feta cheese?

At the other end of the scale, recipes were specially created by world-famous professional chefs many of whose own names or the names of their establishments became synonymous with their classic salads. Caesar Cardini lives on in his inspired, yet simple mixture of crisp leaves, crusty croûtons and tangy Parmesan tossed in a rich, anchovy-flavoured dressing. Serve diced apple, celery and walnuts in a light mayonnaise and you evoke the glamorous style of New York's celebrated Waldorf Astoria hotel.

Classic salads may be simple or luxurious, economical or extravagant. Some are served as a main course, while others make a perfect side dish. They feature ingredients as diverse as beans, pasta, chicken and lobster, but whether they started life in a grand Parisian hotel or an obscure Italian farmhouse, they have stood the test of time and truly become classics.

salad niçoise

ingredients

SERVES 4

2 tuna steaks, about
    2 cm/³/₄ inch thick

olive oil, for brushing

250 g/9 oz green beans,
    topped and tailed

125 ml/4 fl oz vinaigrette or
    garlic vinaigrette dressing

2 hearts of lettuce, leaves
    separated

3 large hard-boiled eggs,
    quartered

2 juicy vine-ripened tomatoes,
    cut into wedges

50 g/1³/₄ oz anchovy fillets in
    oil, drained

55 g/2 oz Niçoise olives,
    stoned

salt and pepper

method

1 Heat a ridged cast-iron griddle pan over a high heat until you can feel the heat rising from the surface. Brush the tuna steaks with oil, place oiled side down on the hot pan, and chargrill for 2 minutes. Lightly brush the top side of the tuna steaks with more oil. Use a pair of tongs to turn the tuna steaks over, then season to taste with salt and pepper. Continue chargrilling for a further 2 minutes for rare or up to 4 minutes for well done. Leave to cool.

2 Meanwhile, bring a saucepan of salted water to the boil. Add the beans to the pan and return to the boil, then boil for 3 minutes, or until tender-crisp. Drain the beans and immediately transfer them to a large bowl. Pour over the vinaigrette and stir together, then leave the beans to cool in the dressing.

3 To serve, line a platter with lettuce leaves. Lift the beans out of the bowl, leaving the excess dressing behind, and pile them in the centre of the platter. Break the tuna into large pieces and arrange it over the beans. Arrange the hard-boiled eggs and tomatoes around the side. Place the anchovy fillets over the salad, then scatter with the olives. Drizzle the remaining dressing over the salad and serve.

chicken, cheese & rocket salad

ingredients

SERVES 4

150 g/5^1/$_2$ oz rocket leaves

2 celery sticks, trimmed and
    sliced

^{1}/$_2$ cucumber, sliced

2 spring onions, trimmed and
    sliced

2 tbsp chopped fresh parsley

25 g/1 oz walnut pieces

350 g/12 oz boneless roast
    chicken, sliced

125 g/4^1/$_2$ oz Stilton cheese,
    cubed

handful of seedless red
    grapes, halved (optional)

salt and pepper

dressing

2 tbsp olive oil

1 tbsp sherry vinegar

1 tsp Dijon mustard

1 tbsp chopped mixed herbs

method

1 Wash the rocket leaves, pat dry with kitchen paper and put them into a large salad bowl. Add the celery, cucumber, spring onions, parsley and walnuts and mix together well. Transfer onto a large serving platter. Arrange the chicken slices over the salad, then scatter over the cheese. Add the red grapes, if using. Season well with salt and pepper.

2 To make the dressing, put all the ingredients into a screw-top jar and shake well. Alternatively, put them into a bowl and mix together well. Drizzle the dressing over the salad and serve.

greek feta salad

ingredients

SERVES 4

a few vine leaves

4 tomatoes, sliced

$^1/_2$ cucumber, peeled and
   sliced

1 small red onion, sliced
   thinly

115 g/4 oz feta cheese, cubed

8 black olives

dressing

3 tbsp extra virgin olive oil

1 tbsp lemon juice

$^1/_2$ tsp dried oregano

salt and pepper

method

1 To make the dressing, put the oil, lemon juice, oregano, and salt and pepper in a screw-top jar and shake together until blended.

2 Arrange the vine leaves on a serving dish and then the tomatoes, cucumber and onion. Scatter the cheese and olives on top. Pour the dressing over the salad and serve.

chef's salad

ingredients

SERVES 6

1 iceberg lettuce, shredded

175 g/6 oz cooked lean ham, cut into thin strips

175 g/6 oz cooked tongue, cut into thin strips

350 g/12 oz cooked chicken, cut into thin strips

175 g/6 oz Gruyère cheese

4 tomatoes, quartered

3 hard-boiled eggs, shelled and quartered

400 ml/14 fl oz Thousand Island dressing

sliced French bread, to serve

method

1 Arrange the lettuce on a large serving platter. Arrange the cold meats decoratively on top.

2 Cut the Gruyère cheese into cubes.

3 Arrange the cheese cubes over the salad, and the tomato and egg quarters around the edge of the platter. Serve the salad immediately with the Thousand Island dressing and sliced French bread.

red onion, tomato & herb salad

ingredients

SERVES 4

900 g/2 lb tomatoes, sliced
    thinly
1 tbsp sugar (optional)
1 red onion, thinly sliced
large handful of finely
    chopped fresh herbs,
    using any in season,
    such as tarragon, sorrel,
    coriander, or basil
salt and pepper

dressing

2–4 tbsp vegetable oil
2 tbsp red wine vinegar or
    fruit vinegar

method

1 Arrange the tomato slices in a shallow bowl. Sprinkle with sugar (if using), and salt and pepper.

2 Separate the onion slices into rings and scatter over the tomatoes. Sprinkle the chopped fresh herbs over the top.

3 Place the dressing ingredients in a jar with a screw-top lid. Shake well. Pour the dressing over the salad and mix gently.

4 Cover with clingfilm and refrigerate for 20 minutes. Remove the salad from the refrigerator 5 minutes before serving, unwrap the dish and stir gently before serving.

caesar salad

ingredients

SERVES 4

4 tbsp olive oil

2 garlic cloves

5 slices white bread,
  crusts removed, cut into
  1-cm/^{1}/$_2$-inch cubes

1 large egg

2 cos lettuce or 3 Little Gem
  lettuce

2 tbsp lemon juice

8 canned anchovy fillets,
  drained and roughly
  chopped

85 g/3 oz fresh Parmesan
  cheese shavings

salt and pepper

method

1 Bring a small, heavy-based saucepan of water to the boil.

2 Meanwhile, make the garlic croûtons. Heat 2 tablespoonfuls of olive oil in a heavy-based frying pan. Add the garlic and diced bread and cook, stirring and tossing frequently, for 4–5 minutes, or until the bread is crispy and golden all over. Remove from the frying pan with a slotted spoon and drain on kitchen paper.

3 While the bread is frying, add the egg to the boiling water and cook for 1 minute, then remove from the saucepan and reserve.

4 Arrange the lettuce leaves in a salad bowl. Mix the remaining olive oil and lemon juice together, then season to taste with salt and pepper. Crack the egg into the dressing and whisk to blend. Pour the dressing over the lettuce leaves, toss well, then add the croûtons and chopped anchovies and toss the salad again. Sprinkle with Parmesan cheese shavings and serve.

tuna & avocado salad

ingredients

SERVES 4

2 avocados, stoned, peeled
    and cubed

250 g/9 oz cherry tomatoes,
    halved

2 red peppers, deseeded and
    chopped

1 bunch fresh flat-leaf
    parsley, chopped

2 garlic cloves, crushed

1 fresh red chilli, deseeded
    and finely chopped

juice of $1/2$ lemon

6 tbsp olive oil

3 tbsp sesame seeds

4 fresh tuna steaks, about
    150 g/$5^1/2$ oz each

8 cooked new potatoes, cubed

pepper

rocket leaves and crusty
    bread, to serve

method

1 Toss the avocados, tomatoes, red peppers, parsley, garlic, chilli, lemon juice and 2 tablespoons of the oil together in a large bowl. Season to taste with pepper, cover and chill in the refrigerator for 30 minutes.

2 Lightly crush the sesame seeds in a mortar with a pestle. Tip the crushed seeds on to a plate and spread out. Press each tuna steak in turn into the crushed seeds to coat on both sides.

3 Heat 2 tablespoons of the remaining oil in a frying pan, add the potatoes and cook, stirring frequently, for 5–8 minutes, or until crisp and brown. Remove from the pan and drain on kitchen paper.

4 Wipe out the pan, add the remaining oil and heat over a high heat until very hot. Add the tuna steaks and cook for 3–4 minutes on each side.

5 To serve, divide the avocado salad between 4 serving plates. Top each with a tuna steak, scatter over the potatoes and rocket leaves and serve with crusty bread.

tomato, mozzarella & avocado salad

ingredients

SERVES 4

2 ripe beef tomatoes

150 g/5^1/$_2$ oz fresh mozzarella

2 avocados

4 tbsp olive oil

1^1/$_2$ tbsp white wine vinegar

1 tsp coarse grain mustard

few fresh basil leaves,
    torn into pieces

20 black olives

salt and pepper

method

1 Using a sharp knife, cut the tomatoes into thick wedges and place in a large serving dish. Drain the mozzarella and roughly tear into pieces. Halve, peel and stone the avocados. Cut the flesh into slices, then arrange the mozzarella cheese and avocado with the tomatoes.

2 Mix the oil, vinegar and mustard together in a small bowl, add salt and pepper to taste, then drizzle over the salad.

3 Scatter the basil and olives over the top and serve immediately.

waldorf summer chicken salad

ingredients

SERVES 4

500 g/1 lb 2 oz red apples, diced

3 tbsp fresh lemon juice

150 ml/5 fl oz mayonnaise

1 head celery

4 shallots, sliced

1 garlic clove, finely chopped

90 g/3$^{1}/_{4}$ oz walnuts, chopped

500 g/1 lb 2 oz cooked chicken, cubed

1 cos lettuce

pepper

method

1 Place the apples in a bowl with the lemon juice and 1 tablespoon of the mayonnaise. Leave for 40 minutes or until required.

2 Slice the celery very thinly. Add the celery with the shallots, garlic and walnuts to the apple, mix and then add the remaining mayonnaise and blend thoroughly.

3 Add the chicken and mix with the other ingredients.

4 Line 4 serving dishes with the lettuce. Pile the chicken salad into the serving dishes, season with pepper and garnish with the chopped walnuts.

warm pasta salad

ingredients

SERVES 4

225 g/8 oz dried farfalle or
    other pasta shapes
6 pieces of sun-dried tomato
    in oil, drained and
    chopped
4 spring onions, chopped
55 g/2 oz rocket, shredded
1/2 cucumber, deseeded and
    diced
salt and pepper

dressing

4 tbsp olive oil
1 tbsp white wine vinegar
1/2 tsp caster sugar
1 tsp Dijon mustard
4 fresh basil leaves, finely
    shredded
salt and pepper

method

1 To make the dressing, whisk the olive oil, vinegar, sugar and mustard together in a jug. Season to taste with salt and pepper and stir in the basil.

2 Bring a large, heavy-based saucepan of lightly salted water to the boil. Add the pasta, return to the boil and cook for 8–10 minutes, or until tender but still firm to the bite. Drain and transfer to a salad bowl. Add the dressing and toss well.

3 Add the tomatoes, spring onions, rocket and cucumber. Season to taste with salt and pepper and toss. Serve warm.

lobster salad

ingredients

SERVES 2

2 raw lobster tails
radicchio leaves
fresh dill sprigs, to garnish

lemon-dill
mayonnaise
4 teaspoons lemon juice
finely grated rind of half a
    lemon
1 large egg yolk
$^{1}/_{2}$ tsp Dijon mustard
150 ml/5 fl oz olive oil
1 tbsp chopped fresh dill
salt and pepper

method

1 To make the lemon-dill mayonnaise, beat the egg yolk in a small bowl, then beat in the mustard and 1 teaspoon of the lemon juice.

2 Using a balloon whisk or electric mixer, beat the oil into the egg yolk mixture, drop by drop, until a thick mayonnaise forms. Stir in the lemon rind and 3 teaspoons of lemon juice.

3 Season the mayonnaise to taste with salt and pepper and add more lemon juice if desired. Stir in the dill, cover and chill in the refrigerator until required.

4 Bring a large saucepan of lightly salted water to the boil. Add the lobster tails, return to the boil and cook for 6 minutes, or until the flesh is opaque and the shells are red. Drain immediately and set aside to cool.

5 Remove the lobster flesh from the shells and cut into bite-sized pieces. Arrange the radicchio leaves on individual plates and top with the lobster flesh. Place a spoonful of the lemon-dill mayonnaise on the side. Garnish with dill sprigs and serve.

salad of greens with lemon dressing

ingredients

SERVES 4

200 g/7 oz mixed baby salad
   leaves such as lamb's
   lettuce, spinach,
   watercress and wild rocket
4 tbsp mixed chopped fresh
   herbs such as flat-leaf
   parsley, mint, coriander
   and basil

dressing

4 tbsp extra virgin olive oil
juice of $^{1}/_{2}$ lemon
1 garlic clove, crushed
salt and pepper

method

1 Wash the salad leaves and discard any thick stalks. Dry and put in a salad bowl. Add the chopped herbs.

2 To make the dressing, mix together the oil, lemon juice, garlic and salt and pepper in a small bowl. Taste and add more oil or lemon juice if necessary.

3 Just before serving, whisk the dressing; pour over the salad leaves, toss and serve.

pasta salad with chargrilled peppers

ingredients

SERVES 4

1 red pepper

1 orange pepper

280 g/10 oz dried conchiglie

5 tbsp extra virgin olive oil

2 tbsp lemon juice

2 tbsp green pesto

1 garlic clove, finely chopped

3 tbsp shredded fresh basil
    leaves

salt and pepper

method

1 Preheat the grill. Put the whole peppers on a baking sheet and place under the hot grill, turning frequently, for 15 minutes, or until charred all over. Remove with tongs and place in a bowl. Cover with crumpled kitchen paper and reserve.

2 Meanwhile, bring a large saucepan of lightly salted water to the boil. Add the pasta, return to the boil and cook for 8–10 minutes, or until the pasta is tender but still firm to the bite.

3 Combine the olive oil, lemon juice, pesto and garlic in a bowl, whisking well to mix. Drain the pasta, add it to the pesto mixture while still hot and toss well. Reserve until required.

4 When the peppers are cool enough to handle, peel off the skins, then cut open and remove the seeds. Chop the flesh roughly and add to the pasta with the basil. Season to taste with salt and pepper and toss well. Serve.

parma ham with melon & asparagus

ingredients

SERVES 4

225 g/8 oz asparagus spears

1 small or $^1/_2$ medium-sized
    Galia or cantaloupe melon

55 g/2 oz Parma ham, thinly
    sliced

150 g/5$^1/_2$ oz bag mixed salad
    leaves, such as herb salad
    with rocket

85 g/3 oz fresh raspberries

1 tbsp fresh Parmesan
    cheese shavings

dressing

1 tbsp balsamic vinegar

2 tbsp raspberry vinegar

2 tbsp orange juice

method

1 Trim the asparagus, cutting in half if very long. Cook in lightly salted, boiling water over a medium heat for 5 minutes, or until tender. Drain and plunge into cold water then drain again and reserve.

2 Cut the melon in half and scoop out the seeds. Cut into small wedges and cut away the rind. Separate the Parma ham slices, cut in half and wrap around the melon wedges.

3 Arrange the salad leaves on a large serving platter and place the melon wedges on top together with the asparagus spears.

4 Scatter over the raspberries and Parmesan cheese shavings. Place the vinegars and juice in a screw-top jar and shake until blended. Pour over the salad and serve.

mushroom salad

ingredients

SERVES 4

225 g/8 oz white or pink
   chestnut mushrooms,
   thinly sliced
finely grated rind and juice of
   $^1/_2$ lemon
3 tbsp crème fraîche
1 tbsp chopped fresh chervil
salt and pepper

method

1 Put the mushrooms in a large bowl, sprinkle with the lemon rind and juice and toss well. Gently stir in the crème fraîche and season with salt and pepper.

2 Cover the bowl with clingfilm and leave to stand, stirring once or twice, for 1 hour. Spoon the salad into a serving bowl, sprinkle with the chervil and serve.

italian salad

ingredients

SERVES 4

225 g/8 oz dried conchiglie

50 g/1¾ oz pine kernels

350 g/12 oz cherry tomatoes, halved

1 red pepper, deseeded and cut into bite-sized chunks

1 red onion, chopped

200 g/7 oz buffalo mozzarella, cubed

12 black olives, stoned

25 g/1 oz fresh basil leaves

fresh Parmesan cheese shavings, to garnish

crusty bread, to serve

dressing

5 tbsp extra virgin olive oil

2 tbsp balsamic vinegar

1 tbsp chopped fresh basil

salt and pepper

method

1 Bring a large saucepan of lightly salted water to the boil. Add the pasta and cook over a medium heat for about 10 minutes, or according to the packet instructions. When cooked, the pasta should be tender but still firm to the bite. Drain, rinse under cold running water and drain again. Leave to cool.

2 While the pasta is cooking, put the pine kernels in a dry frying pan and cook over a low heat for 1–2 minutes until golden brown. Remove from the heat, transfer to a dish and leave to cool.

3 To make the dressing, put the oil, vinegar and basil into a small bowl. Season with salt and pepper and stir together well. Cover with clingfilm and set to one side.

4 To assemble the salad, divide the pasta between serving bowls. Add the pine kernels, tomatoes, red pepper, onion, cheese and olives. Scatter over the basil leaves, then drizzle over the dressing. Garnish with fresh Parmesan cheese shavings and serve with crusty bread.

smoked chicken salad with avocado & tarragon dressing

ingredients

SERVES 4–6

2 large, juicy tomatoes, sliced

600 g/1 lb 5 oz smoked
chicken, skinned and cut
into slices

250 g/9 oz fresh watercress,
any thick stems or yellow
leaves removed, then
rinsed and patted dry

75 g/2¾ oz fresh
beansprouts, soaked for
20 minutes in cold water,
then drained well and
patted dry

leaves from several sprigs
fresh flat-leaf parsley or
coriander

dressing

1 ripe, soft avocado

2 tbsp lemon juice

1 tbsp tarragon vinegar

85 g/3 oz Greek yogurt

1 small garlic clove, crushed

1 tbsp chopped fresh
tarragon leaves

salt and pepper

method

1 To make the dressing, put the avocado,
lemon juice and vinegar in a blender or food
processor and blend until smooth, scraping
down the side with a rubber spatula. Add the
yogurt, garlic and tarragon leaves and process
again. Season with salt and pepper to taste,
then transfer to a bowl. Cover closely with
clingfilm and chill for 2 hours.

2 To assemble the salad, divide the tomato
slices between 4 and 6 individual plates. Toss
the smoked chicken, watercress, beansprouts
and parsley or coriander leaves together. Divide
the salad ingredients between the plates.

3 Adjust the seasoning in the dressing, if
necessary. Spoon the dressing over each
salad and serve.

potato salad

ingredients

SERVES 4

700 g/1 lb 9 oz new potatoes
8 spring onions
250 ml/9 fl oz mayonnaise
1 tsp paprika, plus extra
    pinch to garnish
2 tbsp snipped fresh chives
salt and pepper

method

1 Bring a large saucepan of lightly salted water to the boil. Add the potatoes and cook for 10–15 minutes, or until they are just tender.

2 Drain the potatoes and rinse them under cold running water until completely cold. Drain again. Transfer the potatoes to a bowl and reserve until required.

3 Using a sharp knife, slice the spring onions thinly on the diagonal.

4 Mix the mayonnaise, paprika and salt and pepper to taste together in a bowl. Pour the mixture over the potatoes. Add the spring onions to the potatoes and toss together.

5 Transfer the potato salad to a serving bowl, and sprinkle with snipped chives and a pinch of paprika. Cover and leave to chill in the refrigerator until required.

warm goat's cheese salad

ingredients

SERVES 4

1 small iceberg lettuce, torn
    into pieces
handful of rocket leaves
few radicchio leaves, torn
6 slices French bread
115 g/4 oz goat's cheese,
    sliced

dressing

4 tbsp extra virgin olive oil
1 tbsp white wine vinegar
salt and pepper

method

1 Preheat the grill. Divide all the leaves between 4 individual salad bowls.

2 Toast one side of the bread under the grill until golden. Place a slice of cheese on top of each untoasted side and toast until the cheese is just melting.

3 Put all the dressing ingredients into a bowl and mix together until combined. Pour over the leaves, tossing to coat.

4 Cut each slice of bread in half and place 3 halves on top of each salad. Toss very gently to combine and serve warm.

russian salad

ingredients

SERVES 4

115 g/4 oz new potatoes

115 g/4 oz frozen or shelled
fresh broad beans

115 g/4 oz baby carrots

115 g/4 oz baby sweetcorn

115 g/4 oz baby turnips

115 g/4 oz button
mushrooms, cut into thin
batons

350 g/12 oz cooked peeled
prawns, deveined

125 ml/4 fl oz mayonnaise

1 tbsp lemon juice

2 tbsp bottled capers, drained
and rinsed

2 tbsp extra virgin olive oil

2 hard-boiled eggs, shelled
and halved

4 canned anchovy fillets,
drained and halved

salt and pepper

paprika, to garnish

method

1 Cook the potatoes, broad beans, carrots, sweetcorn and turnips simultaneously. Cook the potatoes in a large saucepan of lightly salted boiling water for 20 minutes. Cook the broad beans in a small saucepan of lightly salted water for 3 minutes, then drain, refresh under cold running water and reserve. Cook the carrots, sweetcorn and turnips in a large saucepan of lightly salted boiling water for 6 minutes.

2 Mix the mushrooms and prawns together in a bowl. Mix the mayonnaise and lemon juice together in a separate bowl, then fold half the mixture into the prawn mixture. Fold in the capers and season to taste with salt and pepper.

3 Drain the mixed vegetables, refresh under cold running water and tip into a bowl. When the potatoes are cooked, drain, refresh under cold running water and tip into the bowl. Pop the broad beans out of their skins by pinching them between your finger and thumb and add to the bowl. Add the olive oil and toss to coat. Divide the potatoes and vegetables between serving plates and top with the prawn mixture. Place a hard-boiled egg half in the centre of each and garnish with the halved anchovies. Dust the eggs with paprika and serve with the remaining mayonnaise mixture.

asparagus & tomato salad

ingredients

SERVES 4

225 g/8 oz asparagus spears

1 lamb's lettuce, washed and torn

25 g/1 oz rocket or mizuna leaves

450 g/1 lb ripe tomatoes, sliced

12 black olives, stoned and chopped

1 tbsp toasted pine kernels

dressing

1 tsp lemon oil

1 tbsp olive oil

1 tsp wholegrain mustard

2 tbsp balsamic vinegar

salt and pepper

method

1 Steam the asparagus spears for about 8 minutes or until tender. Rinse under cold running water to prevent them cooking any further, then cut into 5-cm/2-inch pieces.

2 Arrange the lettuce and rocket leaves around a salad platter to form the base of the salad. Place the sliced tomatoes in a circle on top and the asparagus in the centre.

3 Sprinkle the black olives and pine kernels over the top. To make the dressing, put the lemon oil, olive oil, mustard and vinegar in a screw-top jar and season to taste with salt and pepper. Shake vigorously and drizzle over the salad.

smoked salmon & wild rocket salad

ingredients

SERVES 4

50 g/1³/₄ oz wild rocket leaves
1 tbsp chopped fresh flat-leaf parsley
2 spring onions, finely diced
2 avocados
1 tbsp lemon juice
250 g/9 oz smoked salmon

dressing
150 ml/5 fl oz mayonnaise
2 tbsp lime juice
finely grated rind of 1 lime
1 tbsp chopped fresh flat-leaf parsley, plus extra sprigs to garnish

method

1 Arrange the rocket in 4 individual glass bowls. Scatter over the chopped parsley and spring onions.

2 Halve, peel and stone the avocados and cut into thin slices or small chunks. Brush with the lemon juice to prevent discoloration, then divide between the salad bowls. Mix together gently. Cut the smoked salmon into strips and scatter over the top.

3 Put the mayonnaise in a bowl, then add the lime juice, lime rind and chopped parsley. Mix together well. Spoon some of the mayonnaise dressing on top of each salad and garnish with parsley sprigs.

avocado salad

ingredients

SERVES 4

large handful of radicchio
large handful of rocket
Galia melon
2 ripe avocados
1 tbsp lemon juice
200 g/7 oz fontina cheese,
    cut into bite-sized pieces

dressing

5 tbsp lemon-flavoured or
    extra virgin olive oil
1 tbsp white wine vinegar
1 tbsp lemon juice
1 tbsp chopped fresh parsley,
    plus extra to garnish

method

1 To make the dressing, mix together the oil, vinegar, lemon juice and parsley in a small bowl.

2 Arrange the radicchio and rocket on serving plates. Cut the melon in half and scoop out the seeds. Slice the melon flesh and arrange it over the salad leaves.

3 Halve, peel and stone the avocados. Cut the flesh into slices and brush with lemon juice. Arrange the slices over the melon, then scatter over the cheese. Drizzle over the dressing, garnish with chopped fresh parsley and serve.

three bean salad

ingredients

SERVES 4–6

175 g/6 oz mixed salad
leaves, such as spinach,
rocket and frisée
1 red onion
85 g/3 oz radishes
175 g/6 oz cherry tomatoes
115 g/4 oz cooked beetroot
280 g/10 oz canned
cannellini beans, drained
and rinsed
200 g/7 oz canned red kidney
beans, drained and rinsed
300 g/10½ oz canned
flageolet beans, drained
and rinsed
40 g/1½ oz dried cranberries
55 g/2 oz roasted cashew
nuts
225 g/8 oz feta cheese
(drained weight), crumbled

dressing

4 tbsp extra virgin olive oil
1 tsp Dijon mustard
2 tbsp lemon juice
1 tbsp chopped fresh
coriander
salt and pepper

method

1 Arrange the salad leaves in a salad bowl and reserve.

2 Thinly slice the onion, then cut in half to form half moons and put into a bowl.

3 Thinly slice the radishes, cut the tomatoes in half and peel the beetroot, if necessary, and dice. Add to the onion with the remaining ingredients, except the cranberries, nuts and cheese.

4 Put all the ingredients for the dressing into a screw-top jar and shake until blended. Pour over the bean mixture, toss lightly, then spoon on top of the salad leaves.

5 Scatter over the cranberries, nuts and cheese and serve immediately.

fruit & vegetable salads

For many people, the word salad conjures up a picture of mixed raw vegetables and leaves, perhaps with the addition of olives, beetroot or even fresh herbs, and certainly this is a tasty and healthy combination, but it is rather less than exciting. In fact, vegetable salads are among the most varied and imaginative.

The range of suitable ingredients is vast – from lentils to cauliflower and from peppers to beansprouts – and they can be combined in an almost endless variety of ways, especially if you also include fruit, nuts, cheese or eggs. Salad vegetables don't all have to be raw. Some are best blanched or wilted and then cooled before the salad is assembled, while others benefit from more thorough cooking. Warm salads, where all or some of the ingredients retain some of the heat from being cooked, make especially good starters.

Besides excellent first courses, there are recipes for delicious side dishes and great main course salads for family lunches and informal entertaining. You may even be encouraged to mix and match different dishes for a simple but tempting buffet table. With inspiration for salads from countries as far apart as Greece and Vietnam, you will find an almost limitless source of clever ideas that make vegetable salads an irresistible treat.

green bean salad with feta

ingredients

SERVES 4

350 g/12 oz green beans, trimmed

1 red onion, chopped

3–4 tbsp chopped fresh coriander

2 radishes, thinly sliced

75 g/2¾ oz crumbled feta cheese

1 tsp chopped fresh oregano or ½ tsp dried oregano

2 tbsp red wine or fruit vinegar

5 tbsp extra virgin olive oil

3 ripe tomatoes (optional), cut into wedges

pepper

method

1 Bring about 5 cm/2 inches water to the boil in the base of a steamer or in a medium saucepan. Add the beans to the top of the steamer or place them in a metal colander set over the pan of water. Cover and steam for about 5 minutes, until just tender.

2 Transfer the beans to a bowl and add the onion, coriander, radishes and cheese.

3 Sprinkle the oregano over the salad, then grind pepper over to taste. Whisk the vinegar and olive oil together and pour over the salad. Toss gently to mix well.

4 Transfer to a serving platter, add the tomato wedges, if using, and serve at once or chill until ready to serve.

feta, mint & strawberry salad with green beans & pistachios

ingredients

SERVES 4–6

500 g/1 lb 2 oz fine green
   beans
500 g/1 lb 2 oz strawberries
2–3 tbsp pistachio nuts
1 small bunch fresh mint
   leaves
500 g/1 lb 2 oz feta cheese
   (drained weight)
salt and pepper

dressing

2 tbsp raspberry vinegar
2 tsp caster sugar
1 tbsp Dijon mustard
pinch of salt
125 ml/4 fl oz olive oil

method

1 To make the dressing, mix the vinegar, sugar, mustard and salt together in a bowl until smooth. Slowly pour in the oil, whisking constantly until the mixture has emulsified. Cover and refrigerate until required.

2 Blanch the beans in a large saucepan of salted boiling water for 1–2 minutes, so that they retain plenty of crunch. Drain and quickly toss in a large, cool bowl. Hull and halve the strawberries, then add to the beans. Stir in the pistachio nuts and mint leaves. Toss the salad with enough of the dressing to coat lightly.

3 Break the feta cheese into chunks and scatter over the salad. Add a good grinding of pepper and serve immediately.

herbed mixed bean salad with fried halloumi cheese

ingredients

SERVES 4–6

5 tbsp extra virgin olive oil

2 tbsp tarragon vinegar

$1/2$ tsp mixed grain mustard

pinch of sugar

115 g/4 oz French beans, topped and tailed and cut into bite-sized pieces

115 g/4 oz shelled broad beans, grey outer skins removed if not young

115 g/4 oz fresh or frozen shelled peas

400 g/14 oz canned cannellini beans, drained and rinsed

1 small red onion, thinly sliced

2 tbsp chopped fresh parsley

1 tbsp snipped fresh chives

85 g/3 oz rocket or watercress leaves

salt and pepper

fried halloumi cheese

olive oil

350 g/12 oz halloumi cheese, drained, cut into 12 slices

plain flour, for dusting

method

1 Put the olive oil, vinegar, mustard, sugar and salt and pepper to taste in a small screw-top jar and shake until blended and emulsified. Set aside.

2 Prepare a bowl of iced water. Bring a saucepan of lightly salted water to the boil. Add the French beans and the broad beans and blanch for 3 minutes, or until just tender. Use a slotted spoon to remove the beans from the water and immediately transfer them to the iced water.

3 Return the water to the boil and blanch the peas for 3 minutes, or until tender. Remove from the water and add to the iced water to cool. Drain the beans and peas and pat dry with kitchen paper. Transfer to a large bowl, add the dressing, cannellini beans, onion and herbs and toss. Cover and chill.

4 To make the fried halloumi cheese, heat the oil in a pan over a medium–high heat. Dust the cheese with flour, shaking off the excess and add to the pan. Fry for 3–6 minutes, or until golden. Flip the cheese over and cook the other side, then remove and keep warm while you fry the remaining pieces.

5 Divide the salad ingredients and the rocket leaves between individual plates and arrange the hot cheese alongside. Drizzle the cheese with olive oil and serve.

green & white bean salad

ingredients

SERVES 4

100 g/3^1/$_2$ oz haricot beans,
    soaked overnight
225 g/8 oz fine French beans,
    trimmed
^{1}/$_4$ red onion, thinly sliced
12 black olives, stoned
1 tbsp chopped chives
salt

dressing

^{1}/$_2$ tbsp lemon juice
^{1}/$_2$ tsp Dijon mustard
6 tbsp extra virgin olive oil
salt and pepper

method

1 Drain the haricot beans and put into a saucepan with plenty of fresh water to cover. Bring to the boil, then boil rapidly for 15 minutes. Reduce the heat slightly and cook for a further 30 minutes, or until tender but not disintegrating. Add salt in the last 5 minutes of cooking. Drain and set aside.

2 Meanwhile, plunge the French beans into a large pan of boiling water. Bring back to the boil and cook for 4 minutes, until just tender but still brightly coloured and crunchy. Drain and set aside.

3 Whisk together the dressing ingredients, then leave to stand.

4 While both types of bean are still slightly warm, tip them into a shallow serving dish or arrange on individual plates. Scatter over the onion slices, olives and chives.

5 Whisk the dressing again and spoon over the salad. Serve immediately, at room temperature in a warmed bowl.

broad bean salad

ingredients

SERVES 4

2.5 kg/5 lb 8 oz young broad
  beans in their pods, shelled
  to give about 400 g/14 oz,
  or 425 g/15 oz frozen baby
  broad beans
2 tomatoes, peeled, deseeded
  and diced
3 tbsp shredded basil
50 g/1³/₄ oz fresh Parmesan
  cheese shavings

dressing

1 tsp white wine vinegar
1 small garlic clove, crushed
4 tbsp extra virgin olive oil
salt and pepper

method

1 Bring a large pan of water to a boil. Add the
beans, bring back to the boil, then cook for
3 minutes, until just tender. Drain and tip into
a serving dish or arrange on individual plates.

2 Whisk together the dressing ingredients and
spoon over the beans while still warm.

3 Scatter over the diced tomato, basil and
Parmesan cheese shavings. Serve
immediately, at room temperature in a
warmed bowl.

beansprout salad

ingredients

SERVES 4

350 g/12 oz beansprouts

1 small cucumber

1 green pepper, deseeded
and cut into matchsticks

1 carrot, cut into matchsticks

2 tomatoes, finely chopped

1 celery stick, cut into
matchsticks

fresh chives, to garnish

dressing

1 garlic clove, crushed

dash of chilli sauce

2 tbsp light soy sauce

1 tsp wine vinegar

2 tsp sesame oil

method

1 Blanch the beansprouts in boiling water for 1 minute. Drain well and rinse under cold water. Drain again thoroughly.

2 Cut the cucumber in half lengthways. Scoop out the seeds with a teaspoon and discard. Cut the flesh into matchsticks and mix with the beansprouts, green pepper, carrot, tomatoes and celery.

3 To make the dressing, mix the crushed garlic, chili sauce, soy sauce, wine vinegar and sesame oil in a small bowl.

4 Pour the dressing over the vegetables, tossing well to coat the salad thoroughly.

5 Spoon the salad onto 4 individual serving plates. Garnish with fresh chives and serve immediately.

indonesian warm salad

ingredients

SERVES 4

8 outer leaves of cos lettuce
  or similar dark, crisp
  lettuce leaves

100 g/3^1/$_2$ oz green beans,
  lightly cooked

100 g/3^1/$_2$ oz baby carrots,
  lightly cooked

250 g/9 oz new potatoes,
  cooked until just tender

1 tbsp groundnut oil

125 g/4^1/$_2$ oz fresh
  beansprouts

8-cm/3^1/$_4$-inch piece
  cucumber, deseeded and
  cut into 4-cm/1^1/$_2$-inch
  batons

4 hard-boiled eggs

1 small mild onion, sliced into
  rings

dressing

4 tbsp canned coconut milk

3 tbsp smooth peanut butter

juice of ^{1}/$_2$ lime

2 tsp light soy sauce

dash of Tabasco sauce or any
  chilli sauce

method

1 Roughly tear the lettuce leaves, if large, and arrange on 4 individual serving plates or 1 large serving platter. Halve the cooked beans and cut the cooked carrots, as necessary, into batons. Arrange these with the potatoes (cut into chunks if large) on the plates or platter.

2 Heat the oil in a non-stick frying pan or wok over a high heat, add the beansprouts and stir-fry for 2 minutes until lightly cooked but still crisp. Remove with a slotted spoon and sprinkle over the cooked vegetables with the cucumber. Peel and quarter the eggs, then arrange on top of the salad.

3 Add the onion rings to the oil remaining in the frying pan or wok and stir-fry over a high heat for 5 minutes, or until golden and crisp.

4 Combine all the ingredients for the dressing in a small bowl and pour over the salad. Top with the onion rings and serve immediately.

cauliflower, broccoli & cashew nut salad

ingredients

SERVES 4

2 tbsp groundnut or
  vegetable oil

2 red onions, cut into wedges

1 small head cauliflower,
  cut into florets

1 small head broccoli, cut
  into florets

2 tbsp yellow curry paste or
  red curry paste

400 ml/14 fl oz canned
  coconut milk

1 tsp Thai fish sauce

1 tsp palm sugar or soft, light
  brown sugar

1 tsp salt

85 g/3 oz unsalted cashew
  nuts

handful of fresh coriander,
  chopped, plus extra
  sprigs, torn, to garnish

method

1 Heat the oil in a preheated wok, add the onions and stir-fry over a medium–high heat for 3–4 minutes, until starting to brown. Add the cauliflower and broccoli and stir-fry for 1–2 minutes. Stir in the curry paste and stir-fry for 30 seconds, then add the coconut milk, fish sauce, sugar and salt. Bring gently to the boil, stirring occasionally, then reduce the heat and simmer gently for 3–4 minutes, until the vegetables are almost tender.

2 Meanwhile, heat a separate dry frying pan until hot, add the cashew nuts and cook, shaking the pan frequently, for 2–3 minutes, until lightly browned. Add to the stir-fry with the coriander, stir well and serve immediately, garnished with the torn coriander sprigs.

lentil & goat's cheese salad

ingredients

SERVES 4

25 g/1 oz Puy lentils

1 bay leaf

2 spring onions, finely
chopped

50 g /1³/4 oz red pepper,
deseeded and diced

15 ml/1 tbsp chopped fresh
parsley

100 g/3¹/2 oz cherry
tomatoes, sliced in half

50 g/1³/4 oz rocket

30 g/1¹/3 oz goat's cheese,
sliced or crumbled

dressing

5 ml/1 tsp olive oil

5 ml/1 tsp balsamic vinegar

2.5 ml/¹/2 tsp runny honey

1 clove garlic, peeled and
crushed or finely chopped

method

1 Rinse the lentils and put in a medium-sized
saucepan. Add the bay leaf and cover with
plenty of cold water, bring to the boil then
reduce the heat and simmer for 20–30 minutes,
or until the lentils are tender.

2 Drain the lentils and transfer to a bowl. Add
the spring onions, red pepper, parsley and
cherry tomatoes. Mix well.

3 To make the dressing, whisk together the oil,
vinegar, honey and garlic in a bowl and stir
into the lentils.

fruity cottage cheese salad

ingredients

SERVES 4

85 g/3 oz cottage cheese

1 tsp chopped fresh parsley

1 tbsp snipped fresh chives

1 tsp chopped fresh chervil or basil

2 assorted coloured peppers, deseeded and peeled

1 small melon, such as Ogen (about 300 g/10^1/$_2$ oz after peeling and deseeding)

175 g/6 oz assorted salad leaves

55 g/2 oz seedless grapes

1 red onion, thinly sliced

dressing

3 tbsp freshly squeezed lime juice

1 small fresh red chilli, deseeded and finely chopped

1 tsp clear honey

1 tbsp soy sauce

method

1 Place the cottage cheese in a bowl and stir in the chopped herbs. Cover lightly and reserve.

2 Cut the peeled peppers into thin strips and reserve. Cut the melon in half and scoop out the seeds. Slice the melon flesh into small wedges.

3 Arrange the salad leaves on a large serving platter with the melon wedges.

4 Spoon the herb-flavoured cottage cheese on the platter and arrange the reserved peppers, grapes and red onion slices around the cheese.

5 To make the dressing, mix the lime juice, chilli, honey and soy sauce together in a small bowl or jug then drizzle over the salad and serve as 4 portions.

warm asian-style salad

ingredients

SERVES 4

115 g/4 oz broccoli florets

115 g/4 oz baby carrots,
    scraped and cut in half
    lengthways

140 g/5 oz pak choi

1 tbsp sunflower oil

1 red onion, sliced

1–2 fresh bird's eye chillies,
    deseeded and sliced

2.5-cm/1-inch fresh ginger,
    peeled and grated

2 whole star anise

1 red pepper, deseeded and
    cut into strips

1 orange pepper, deseeded
    and cut into strips

115 g/4 oz baby courgettes,
    trimmed and sliced
    diagonally

115 g/4 oz baby sweetcorn,
    sliced in half lengthways

2 tbsp orange juice

1 tbsp soy sauce

1 tbsp cashew nuts

method

1 Cut the broccoli into tiny florets then bring a small saucepan of water to the boil and add the halved carrots. Cook for 3 minutes then add the broccoli and cook for a further 2 minutes. Drain and plunge into cold water then drain again and reserve.

2 Arrange 25 g/1 oz of pak choi on a large serving platter. Shred the remainder and set aside.

3 Heat a wok and when hot, add the oil and heat for 30 seconds. Add the sliced onion, chillies, ginger and star anise and stir-fry for 1 minute. Add the pepper strips, courgettes and baby sweetcorn and stir-fry for a further 2 minutes.

4 Pour in the orange juice and soy sauce and continue to stir-fry for a further 1 minute before adding the reserved shredded pak choi, broccoli and carrots. Stir-fry for 2 minutes, or until the vegetables are tender but still firm to the bite. Arrange the warm salad on the pak choi-lined serving platter, scatter the cashew nuts over the top and serve as 4 portions.

moroccan tomato & red pepper salad

ingredients

SERVES 4

3 red peppers

4 ripe tomatoes

1/2 bunch of fresh coriander, chopped

2 garlic cloves, finely chopped

salt and pepper

method

1 Preheat the grill. Place the peppers on a baking sheet and cook under the grill, turning occasionally, for 15 minutes. Add the tomatoes and grill, turning occasionally, for a further 5–10 minutes, or until all the skins are charred and blistered. Remove from the heat and leave to cool.

2 Peel and deseed the peppers and tomatoes and slice the flesh thinly. Place in a bowl, mix well and season with salt and pepper. Sprinkle with the coriander and garlic, cover with clingfilm and chill in the refrigerator for at least 1 hour. Just before serving, drain off any excess liquid.

wilted spinach, yogurt & walnut salad

ingredients

SERVES 2

450 g/1 lb fresh spinach
　　leaves
1 onion, chopped
1 tbsp olive oil
225 ml/8 fl oz natural yogurt
1 garlic clove, finely chopped
2 tbsp chopped toasted
　　walnuts
2–3 tsp chopped fresh mint
salt and pepper
pitta bread, to serve

method

1 Rinse the spinach and place in a non stick pan with the water that clings to the leaves. Add the onions and cook gently over a low heat, until the spinach has wilted.

2 Add the oil and cook for a further 5 minutes. Season to taste with salt and pepper.

3 Combine the yogurt and garlic in a bowl.

4 Put the spinach and onion into a serving bowl and pour over the yogurt mixture. Scatter over the walnuts and chopped mint and serve with pitta bread.

moroccan carrot & orange salad

ingredients

SERVES 4

450 g/1 lb carrots, peeled

1 tbsp olive oil

2 tbsp lemon juice

pinch of granulated sugar

2 large oranges, peeled and cut into segments (reserve any juice)

55 g/2 oz raisins

1 tsp ground cinnamon

2 tbsp toasted pine kernels

method

1 Grate the carrots into a large bowl.

2 In a separate bowl, combine the oil, lemon juice, sugar and any orange juice reserved from the preparing of the orange segments.

3 Toss the orange segments with the carrots and stir in the raisins and cinnamon.

4 Pour over the dressing and scatter over the pine kernels just before serving.

hot tomato & basil salad

ingredients

SERVES 6

700 g/1 lb 9 oz cherry
    tomatoes
1 garlic clove, crushed
2 tbsp capers, drained and
    rinsed
1 tsp granulated sugar
4 tbsp olive oil
2 tbsp torn fresh basil

method

1 Preheat the oven to 200°C/400°F/Gas Mark 6. Stir the tomatoes, garlic, capers and sugar together in a bowl and tip into a roasting tin.

2 Pour over the oil and toss to coat.

3 Cook in the oven for 10 minutes until the tomatoes are hot.

4 Remove from the oven and tip into a heatproof serving bowl. Scatter over the basil and serve immediately.

sweet & sour cabbage salad

ingredients

SERVES 6

125 ml/4 fl oz fish sauce

125 ml/4 fl oz freshly
squeezed lime juice

100 g/3^1/$_2$ oz palm sugar or
granulated sugar

2 tbsp vegetable oil

3 red bird's eye chillies,
deseeded and thinly sliced
into rounds

1 small green cabbage, finely
shredded

2 large carrots, cut into
matchsticks

1 small red onion, finely
sliced

12 basil leaves, freshly torn

method

1 Put the fish sauce, lime juice and sugar in a
non-metallic bowl and whisk until the sugar is
completely dissolved. Add the oil, chillies,
cabbage, carrots and onion. Toss well and
leave to stand for 30 minutes to 1 hour.

2 Drain and serve scattered with the basil.

green pawpaw salad

ingredients

SERVES 6

125 ml/4 fl oz freshly
squeezed lime juice

100 ml/3¹/₂ fl oz fish sauce

60 g/2¹/₄ oz palm sugar or
granulated sugar

1 large green pawpaw,
peeled, deseeded and cut
into very thin matchsticks

2 small carrots, peeled and
cut into matchsticks

3 red bird's eye chillies,
deseeded and thinly sliced
into rounds

75 g/2³/₄ oz dry-roasted,
unsalted peanuts,
chopped

8 g/1/6 oz fresh coriander,
finely chopped

method

1 Put the lime juice, fish sauce and sugar in a
non-reactive bowl and whisk until the sugar is
completely dissolved. Add the pawpaw,
carrots and chillies. Toss well and leave to
stand for 30 minutes.

2 Drain and serve scattered with the peanuts
and coriander.

tomato salad with fried feta

ingredients

SERVES 4

12 tomatoes, sliced

1 very small red onion, sliced
    very thinly

15 g/^{1}/$_2$ oz rocket leaves

20 black olives, stoned

200 g/7 oz feta cheese

1 egg

3 tbsp plain white flour

2 tbsp olive oil

dressing

3 tbsp extra virgin olive oil

juice of ^{1}/$_2$ lemon

2 tsp chopped fresh oregano

pinch of sugar

pepper

method

1 Make the dressing by whisking together the extra virgin olive oil, the lemon juice, oregano, sugar and pepper in a small bowl. Set aside.

2 Prepare the salad by arranging the tomatoes, onion, rocket and olives on 4 individual plates.

3 Cut the feta cheese into cubes about 2.5 cm/1 inch square. Beat the egg in a dish and put the flour on a separate plate. Toss the cheese first in the egg, shake off the excess, and then toss in the flour.

4 Heat the olive oil in a large frying pan, add the cheese and fry over a medium heat, turning over the cubes of cheese until they are golden on all sides.

5 Scatter the fried feta over the salad. Whisk together the prepared dressing, spoon over the salad and serve warm.

orange & olive salad

ingredients

SERVES 4

4 thick-skinned oranges

1 small red onion, sliced very
     thinly

16 black olives, stoned

2 tbsp extra virgin olive oil

1 tbsp lemon juice

pinch of sugar

lettuce leaves, to serve

chopped fresh herbs such as
     flat-leaf parsley, mint or
     dill, to garnish

salt and pepper

method

1 Using a sharp knife, remove the peel and pith from the oranges then cut the flesh into thin 5-mm/1/4-inch thick slices, discarding the seeds and white membrane. Put the oranges and any juice, the onion slices and the olives in a large bowl.

2 To make the dressing, whisk together the oil, lemon juice, sugar, salt and pepper to taste and drizzle over the oranges, onion slices and olives. Gently toss together then chill in the fridge for 2–3 hours before serving in a shallow dish lined with lettuce leaves. Garnish with chopped fresh herbs.

charred pepper salad

ingredients

SERVES 4–6

2 green peppers

2 red peppers

2 yellow peppers

$^{1}/_{2}$ tsp cumin seeds or 2 tbsp
chopped fresh marjoram

5 tbsp extra virgin olive oil

2 tbsp lemon juice

2 garlic cloves, crushed

pinch of sugar

salt and pepper

black olives, stoned, to
garnish

method

1 Preheat the grill. Cook the peppers under the grill, turning frequently, until the skins are charred all over. Put the peppers in a bowl, cover with a damp tea towel and leave until cold.

2 When the peppers are cold, hold them over a clean bowl to collect the juices and peel off the skin. Remove the stem, core and seeds and cut the peppers into thin strips. Arrange the pepper strips on a flat serving plate.

3 If using cumin seeds, dry-toast them in a dry frying pan until they turn brown and begin to pop. Shake the frying pan continuously to prevent them from burning and do not allow them to smoke. Lightly crush the toasted seeds with a pestle and mortar.

4 Add the toasted cumin seeds or marjoram, the olive oil, lemon juice, garlic, sugar, salt and pepper to the pepper juices and whisk together.

5 Pour the dressing over the peppers and chill in the fridge for 3–4 hours or overnight. Serve at room temperature, garnished with olives.

hot-&-sour vegetable salad

ingredients

SERVES 4

2 tbsp vegetable or
    groundnut oil

1 tbsp chilli oil

1 onion, sliced

2.5-cm/1-inch piece ginger,
    grated

1 small head broccoli,
    cut into florets

2 carrots, cut into
    matchsticks

1 red pepper, deseeded and
    cut into squares

1 yellow pepper, deseeded
    and cut into strips

50 g/1³/₄ oz mangetout,
    trimmed and halved

50 g/1³/₄ oz baby sweetcorn,
    halved

dressing

2 tbsp vegetable or
    groundnut oil

1 tsp chilli oil

1 tbsp rice wine vinegar

juice of 1 lime

¹/₂ tsp fish sauce

method

1 Heat the oils in a wok or large frying pan and
fry the onion and ginger for 1–2 minutes until
they start to soften. Add the vegetables and
stir-fry for 2–3 minutes until they have softened
slightly. Remove from the heat and set aside.

2 Mix the dressing ingredients together. Transfer
the vegetables to a serving plate and drizzle
the dressing over. Serve warm immediately, or
allow the flavours to develop and serve cold.

curried egg salad

ingredients

SERVES 4

6 eggs

1 tbsp vegetable or
    groundnut oil

1 onion, chopped

1 tbsp yellow curry paste

4 tbsp natural yogurt

1/2 tsp salt

handful of fresh coriander,
    chopped finely

bunch of watercress

2 courgettes, cut into
    matchsticks

1 fresh green chilli, deseeded
    and chopped finely

1 tsp fish sauce

1 tsp rice wine vinegar

3 tbsp vegetable or
    groundnut oil

method

1 Put the eggs in a saucepan, cover with cold water and bring to the boil. Simmer for 10 minutes, then drain and rinse in cold water. Shell and halve.

2 Meanwhile, heat the oil in a medium frying pan and fry the onion gently until softened but not browned. Remove from the heat and stir in the curry paste. Cool slightly before stirring in the yogurt, salt and half the coriander. Set aside.

3 Arrange the watercress and courgettes on a platter. Mix the chilli, fish sauce, vinegar and oil together and pour the dressing over the leaves.

4 Arrange the eggs on top and spoon the yogurt mixture over each one. Garnish with the remaining coriander and serve immediately.

julienne vegetable salad

ingredients

SERVES 4

4 tbsp vegetable or
    groundnut oil
225 g/8 oz tofu with herbs,
    cubed
1 red onion, sliced
4 spring onions, cut into
    5-cm/2-inch lengths
1 garlic clove, chopped
2 carrots, cut into
    matchsticks
115 g/4 oz fine French beans,
    trimmed
1 yellow pepper, deseeded
    and cut into strips
115 g/4 oz broccoli, cut into
    florets
1 large courgette, cut into
    matchsticks
50 g/1³/₄ oz beansprouts
2 tbsp red curry paste
4 tbsp soy sauce
1 tbsp rice wine vinegar
1 tsp palm sugar or soft,
    light brown sugar
few basil leaves, plus extra to
    garnish (optional)
350 g/12 oz rice vermicelli
    noodles

method

1 Heat the oil in a wok or large frying pan and fry the tofu cubes for 3–4 minutes, until browned on all sides. Lift out of the oil and drain on kitchen paper.

2 Add the onions, garlic and carrots to the hot oil and fry for 1–2 minutes before adding the rest of the vegetables, except for the beansprouts. Stir-fry for 2–3 minutes. Add the beansprouts, then stir in the curry paste, soy, vinegar, sugar and basil leaves. Cook for 30 seconds.

3 Soak the noodles in boiling water or stock for 2–3 minutes (check the packet instructions) or until tender and drain well.

4 Pile the vegetables onto the noodles, and serve topped with the tofu cubes. Garnish with extra basil, if using.

aubergine & onion salad

ingredients

SERVES 4

4 tbsp vegetable or
    groundnut oil

1 onion, sliced

4 shallots, chopped finely

4 spring onions, sliced

350 g/12 oz aubergines,
    cubed

2 tbsp green curry paste

2 tbsp soy sauce

1 tsp palm sugar or soft, light
    brown sugar

115 g/4 oz creamed coconut,
    chopped

3 tbsp water

small handful of fresh
    coriander, chopped

few basil leaves, chopped

small handful of fresh parsley,
    chopped

115 g/4 oz rocket leaves

2 tbsp sweet chilli sauce

method

1 Heat half the oil in a wok or large frying pan
and fry all the onions together for 1–2 minutes,
until just softened but not browned. Lift out
and reserve.

2 Fry the aubergine cubes, in batches if
necessary, adding more oil as needed, until
they are crisp and golden brown.

3 Return the onions to the wok and add the
curry paste, soy sauce and sugar. Add the
creamed coconut and water, and cook until
dissolved. Stir in most of the coriander, the
basil and parsley.

4 Toss the rocket in the chilli sauce and serve
with the aubergine and onion salad. Garnish
with the remaining herbs.

chinese tomato salad

ingredients

SERVES 4

2 large tomatoes

dressing

1 tbsp finely chopped spring
   onion

1 tsp finely chopped garlic

$1/2$ tsp sesame oil

1 tbsp white rice vinegar

$1/2$ tsp salt

pinch of white pepper

pinch of sugar

method

1 Mix together all the ingredients for the dressing and reserve.

2 Thinly slice the tomatoes. Arrange on a plate and pour the dressing over the top.

beetroot salad

ingredients

SERVES 4–6

900 g/2 lb raw beetroots
4 tbsp extra virgin olive oil
1½ tbsp red wine vinegar
2 garlic cloves, finely chopped
2 spring onions, very finely
    chopped
coarse sea salt

method

1 Carefully remove the roots from the beetroots without cutting into the skin, then cut off all but 2.5 cm/1 inch of the stalks. Gently rub the beetroots under cold running water, without splitting the skins, to remove any dirt.

2 Put the beetroots in a saucepan with water to cover and bring to the boil. Cover, reduce the heat slightly and cook for 25–40 minutes, depending on the size, until the largest beetroot is tender when you pierce it with a long metal skewer or knife.

3 Meanwhile, put the oil, vinegar, garlic, spring onions and salt to taste in a jar with a screw-top lid and shake until emulsified, then set aside.

4 Drain the beetroots and rinse under cold running water until cool enough to handle, then peel away the skins. Thickly chop or slice the beetroots, then put in a bowl and pour over the dressing. Cover and chill in the refrigerator for at least 1 hour.

5 To serve, gently toss the salad and transfer to a serving platter.

watercress, courgette & mint salad

ingredients

SERVES 4

2 courgettes, cut into batons
100 g/3¹/₂ oz green beans,
　　cut into thirds
1 green pepper, deseeded
　　and cut into strips
2 celery sticks, sliced
1 bunch watercress

dressing

200 ml/7 fl oz natural yogurt
1 garlic clove, crushed
2 tbsp chopped fresh mint
pepper

method

1 Bring a saucepan of lightly salted water to the boil, add the courgette batons and beans and cook for 7–8 minutes. Drain, rinse under cold running water and drain again. Set aside to cool completely.

2 Mix the courgettes and beans with the pepper strips, celery and watercress in a large serving bowl.

3 To make the dressing, combine the yogurt, garlic and mint in a small bowl. Season with pepper to taste.

4 Spoon the dressing on to the salad and serve immediately.

poultry & meat salads

There is a world of difference between serving, say, chicken with salad and creating a genuine chicken salad. For a truly delicious, attractive and appetizing dish, the meat or poultry needs to be an integral part of the salad and combine perfectly with the other ingredients, whether vegetables, nuts, herbs, fruit, pasta or rice.

Virtually all kinds of poultry and meat make terrific salads. Chicken and turkey go especially well with creamy mixtures, duck is delicious with piquant flavours, bacon and pancetta have a natural affinity with peppery leaves and the earthy taste of mushrooms, while beef works equally well with both Western and Eastern culinary traditions. Duck, bacon and beef, in particular, are superb in warm salads.

Serving a main course salad made with meat or poultry is not only a good way to add variety to the family menu in the winter as well as the summer, but also an easy route to a healthy diet. You are more or less guaranteed a balanced and nutritious meal with protein, vitamins, minerals, fibre and, if the salad includes potatoes, noodles, pasta or rice, carbohydrates too. If not, serve it with crusty rolls or fresh bread – delicious.

chicken avocado salad

ingredients

SERVES 4

4 large handfuls mixed salad
  leaves, such as beetroot
  greens, escarole, endive
  and radicchio

400 g/14 oz boneless cooked
  chicken, shredded

2 satsumas, separated into
  segments

2 celery sticks, thinly sliced

1/2 red onion, halved and
  thinly sliced

2 tbsp snipped fresh chives

2 avocados

salt and pepper

2 tbsp toasted sunflower
  seeds, to garnish

pitta bread, to serve

dressing

125 ml/4 fl oz extra virgin
  olive oil

3 tbsp Chinese rice wine
  vinegar

1/2 tsp Dijon mustard

pinch of caster sugar

method

1 To make the dressing, put the olive oil,
vinegar, mustard, sugar and salt and pepper
to taste into a small screw-top jar and shake
until blended and emulsified.

2 Put the salad leaves into a bowl, add about
one-third of the dressing and lightly toss. Add
the chicken, satsumas, celery, onion, chives
and the remaining dressing and toss again.

3 Halve, peel and stone the avocados. Cut the
flesh into thin slices, add to the other
ingredients and gently toss together, making
sure the avocado slices are completely coated
with dressing so they don't discolour.

4 Arrange on individual plates, sprinkle with
the sunflower seeds and serve with pitta bread
on the side.

cajun chicken salad

ingredients

SERVES 4

4 skinless, boneless chicken
    breasts, about 140 g/5 oz
    each
4 tsp Cajun seasoning
2 tsp sunflower oil (optional)
1 ripe mango, peeled, stoned
    and cut into thick slices
200 g/7 oz mixed salad leaves
1 red onion, thinly sliced and
    cut in half
175 g/6 oz cooked beetroot,
    diced
85 g/3 oz radishes, sliced
55 g/2 oz walnut halves
2 tbsp sesame seeds,
    to garnish

dressing

4 tbsp walnut oil
1–2 tsp Dijon mustard
1 tbsp lemon juice
salt and pepper

method

1 Make 3 diagonal slashes across each chicken breast. Put the chicken into a shallow dish and sprinkle all over with the Cajun seasoning. Cover and refrigerate for at least 30 minutes.

2 When ready to cook, brush a griddle pan with the sunflower oil, if using. Heat over a high heat until very hot and a few drops of water sprinkled into the pan sizzle immediately. Add the chicken and cook for 7–8 minutes on each side, or until thoroughly cooked. If still slightly pink in the centre, cook a little longer. Remove the chicken and reserve.

3 Add the mango slices to the pan and cook for 2 minutes on each side. Remove and reserve.

4 Meanwhile, arrange the salad leaves in a salad bowl and scatter over the onion, beetroot, radishes and walnut halves.

5 Put the walnut oil, mustard, lemon juice and salt and pepper to taste in a screw-top jar and shake until well blended. Pour over the salad.

6 Arrange the mango and the salad on the serving plate, top with the chicken breast and sprinkle with sesame seeds.

roast chicken with pesto cream salad

ingredients

SERVES 4–6

600 g/1 lb 5 oz cooked
   boneless chicken, any
   skin removed and cut into
   bite-sized pieces
3 celery sticks, chopped
2 large skinned red peppers
   from a jar, well drained
   and sliced
salt and pepper
iceberg lettuce leaves,
   to serve

pesto cream

150 ml/5 fl oz crème fraîche
about 4 tbsp bottled pesto

method

1 To make the pesto cream, put the crème fraîche into a large bowl, then beat in 4 tablespoons pesto. Taste and add more pesto if you want a stronger flavour.

2 Add the chicken, celery and red peppers to the bowl and gently toss together. Add salt and pepper to taste and toss again. Cover and chill until required.

3 Remove the salad from the refrigerator 10 minutes before serving to return to room temperature. Give the salad ingredients a good stir, then divide between individual plates lined with lettuce leaves.

braised chicken salad

ingredients

SERVES 4

3 tbsp olive oil

1 chicken, weighing about
    1.3 kg/3 lb

200 ml/7 fl oz dry white wine

1 onion, chopped

1 carrot, chopped

1 celery stalk, chopped

1 fresh bay leaf

salt and pepper

marinade

1 tsp black peppercorns

4 fresh bay leaves

125 ml/4 fl oz olive oil

salt

salad

150 g/5 1/2 oz baby spinach
    leaves

5 tender celery stalks

1 head chicory

1 tsp wine vinegar

1 tsp balsamic vinegar

salt

method

1 Preheat the oven to 180°C/350°F/Gas Mark 4.
Heat the olive oil in an ovenproof casserole
over medium–high heat. Add the chicken and
fry for 15 minutes, turning, until golden all over.
Pour in the wine and simmer for 2 minutes,
then add the onion, carrot, celery and bay leaf.
Season with salt and pepper. Cover tightly and
transfer to the oven. Bake for 45–50 minutes,
turning every 20 minutes, until the juices from
the thickest part of the thigh run clear when
pierced with a skewer. Remove the chicken
from the pan to cool. When cool enough to
handle, remove and discard the skin. Strip the
meat from the bone, slicing any large chunks
into bite-sized pieces.

2 Arrange the chicken in a dish. Sprinkle with
salt, a few peppercorns and the bay leaves.
Pour in enough oil to generously coat. Cover
tightly with clingfilm and marinate in the
refrigerator for 1–2 days. Remove the chicken
from the fridge 2 hours before serving. Place
in a colander set over a bowl to drain, and
leave to stand until the oil has liquefied.

3 To make the salad, chop the leaves as
desired. Combine the spinach, celery and
chicory in a large serving dish. Toss with salt,
enough oil from the chicken to just coat the
leaves, and the wine vinegar. Arrange the
chicken on top, discarding the peppercorns
and bay leaves. Sprinkle with the balsamic
vinegar before serving.

thai chicken salad

ingredients

SERVES 6

1 tbsp sunflower oil

115 g/4 oz skinless chicken
breast, cut lengthways
horizontally

25 g/1 oz rice vermicelli

shop bought spicy dressing of
your choice

3 limes, halved

salad

50 g /1^3/$_4$ oz deseeded mixed
peppers, finely sliced into
strips

50 g /1^3/$_4$ oz, peeled weight,
carrot, finely sliced into
strips

50 g/1^3/$_4$ oz courgette, finely
sliced into strips

50 g/1^3/$_4$ oz mangetout, finely
sliced into strips

50 g/1^3/$_4$ oz baby corn cobs,
finely sliced into strips

50 g/1^3/$_4$ oz broccoli florets,
cut into 5-mm/^{1}/$_4$-inch
pieces

50 g/1^3/$_4$ oz pak choi,
shredded

60 ml/4 tbsp roughly
chopped fresh coriander
leaves

method

1 Heat a griddle pan over a high heat and brush lightly with oil. Add the chicken and cook for 2 minutes on each side, or until thoroughly cooked through. Remove the chicken from the pan and shred.

2 Cook the vermicelli according to the packet instructions.

3 To make the salad, put all the salad ingredients with the chicken into a large bowl. Pour over the dressing and toss together, making sure that all the ingredients are well coated.

4 Cover and refrigerate for at least 2 hours before serving. Serve on large plates, squeezing the juice from half a lime over each portion.

layered chicken salad

ingredients

SERVES 4

750 g/1 lb 10 oz new
    potatoes, scrubbed

1 red pepper, halved and
    deseeded

1 green pepper, halved and
    deseeded

2 small courgettes, sliced

1 small onion, thinly sliced

3 tomatoes, sliced

350 g/12 oz cooked chicken,
    sliced

snipped fresh chives,
    to garnish

dressing

150 ml/5 fl oz natural yogurt

3 tbsp mayonnaise

1 tbsp snipped fresh chives

salt and pepper

method

1 Put the potatoes into a large saucepan, add just enough cold water to cover and bring to the boil. Lower the heat, cover and simmer for 15–20 minutes until tender. Meanwhile, place the pepper halves, skin side up, under a preheated hot grill and grill until the skins blacken and begin to char.

2 Remove the peppers with tongs, place in a bowl and cover with clingfilm. Set aside until cool enough to handle, then peel off the skins and slice the flesh.

3 Bring a small pan of lightly salted water to the boil. Add the courgettes, bring back to the boil and simmer for 3 minutes. Drain, rinse under cold running water to prevent any further cooking and drain again. Set aside.

4 To make the dressing, whisk the yogurt, mayonnaise and snipped chives together in a small bowl until well blended. Season to taste with salt and pepper.

5 When the potatoes are tender, drain, cool and slice them. Add them to the dressing and mix gently to coat evenly. Spoon the potatoes on to 4 serving plates, dividing them equally.

6 Top each plate with one quarter of the pepper slices and courgettes. Layer one quarter of the onion and tomato slices, then the sliced chicken, on top of each serving. Garnish with snipped chives and serve immediately.

turkey salad pitta

ingredients

MAKES 1

small handful baby leaf
  spinach, rinsed, patted dry
  and shredded

$^1/_2$ red pepper, deseeded and
  thinly sliced

$^1/_2$ carrot, peeled and coarsely
  grated

4 tbsp hummus

85 g/3 oz boneless, skinless
  cooked turkey meat, thinly
  sliced

$^1/_2$ tbsp toasted sunflower
  seeds

1 wholemeal pitta bread

salt and pepper

method

1 Preheat the grill to high.

2 Put the spinach leaves, red pepper, carrot and hummus into a large bowl and stir together, so all the salad ingredients are coated with the hummus. Stir in the turkey and sunflower seeds and season with salt and pepper to taste.

3 Put the pitta bread under the grill for about 1 minute on each side to warm through, but do not brown. Cut it in half to make 2 'pockets' of bread.

4 Divide the salad between the bread pockets and serve.

turkey & rice salad

ingredients

SERVES 4

1 litre/1³/₄ pints chicken stock
175 g/6 oz mixed long-grain
    and wild rice
2 tbsp sunflower or corn oil
225 g/8 oz skinless, boneless
    turkey breast, trimmed of
    all visible fat and cut into
    thin strips
225 g/8 oz mangetout
115 g/4 oz oyster mushrooms,
    torn into pieces
55 g/2 oz shelled pistachio
    nuts, finely chopped
2 tbsp chopped fresh
    coriander
1 tbsp snipped fresh garlic
    chives
salt and pepper
1 tbsp balsamic vinegar
fresh garlic chives, to garnish

method

1 Reserve 3 tablespoons of the chicken stock and bring the remainder to the boil in a large saucepan. Add the rice and cook for 30 minutes, or until tender. Drain and leave to cool slightly.

2 Meanwhile, heat 1 tablespoon of the oil in a preheated wok or frying pan. Stir-fry the turkey over a medium heat for 3–4 minutes, or until cooked through. Using a slotted spoon, transfer the turkey to a dish. Add the mangetout and mushrooms to the wok and stir-fry for 1 minute. Add the reserved stock, bring to the boil, then reduce the heat, cover and simmer for 3–4 minutes. Transfer the vegetables to the dish and leave to cool slightly.

3 Thoroughly mix the rice, turkey, mangetout, mushrooms, nuts, coriander and garlic chives together, then season to taste with salt and pepper. Drizzle with the remaining sunflower oil and the vinegar and garnish with fresh garlic chives. Serve warm.

warm duck salad

ingredients

SERVES 4

175 g/6 oz duck breast,
    all fat removed

2 tbsp sunflower oil

2.5-cm/1-inch piece fresh
    ginger, peeled and grated

1 fresh red chilli, deseeded
    and sliced

1 red onion, cut into thin
    wedges

2 celery sticks, trimmed and
    finely sliced

1 small red pepper, deseeded
    and finely sliced

1 tbsp soy sauce

115 g/4 oz courgettes,
    trimmed and sliced

2 ripe but still firm plums,
    stoned and sliced

85 g/3 oz pak choi, sliced

1 tbsp chopped fresh
    coriander

method

1 Cut the duck breast into thin strips and
reserve. Heat a wok until very hot then spray
with the oil and heat for 30 seconds. Add
the ginger, chilli and duck strips and stir-fry
for 1–2 minutes, or until the duck strips
are browned.

2 Add the onion wedges and celery and pepper
slices and continue to stir-fry for 3 minutes.

3 Add the soy sauce, courgettes and plums to
the wok and stir-fry for 2 minutes before stirring
in the shredded pak choi and the chopped
coriander. Stir-fry for a further minute then
serve, divided equally between 4 bowls.

asian duck & noodle salad with peanut sauce

ingredients

SERVES 3

2 carrots, peeled

2 celery sticks

1 cucumber

three 140-g/5-oz duck breasts

350 g/12 oz rice noodles, cooked according to the instructions on the packet, rinsed and drained

peanut sauce

2 garlic cloves, crushed

2 tbsp dark brown sugar

2 tbsp peanut butter

2 tbsp coconut cream

2 tbsp soy sauce

2 tbsp rice vinegar

2 tbsp sesame oil

$^1/_2$ tsp freshly ground black pepper

$^1/_2$ tsp Chinese five-spice powder

$^1/_2$ tsp ground ginger

method

1 Preheat the grill. Cut the carrots, celery and cucumber into thin strips and set aside.

2 Grill the duck breasts for about 5 minutes on each side until cooked through. Leave to cool.

3 Meanwhile, heat all the ingredients for the sauce in a small saucepan until combined and the sugar has dissolved completely. Stir until smooth.

4 Slice the duck breasts. Divide the noodles among 3 serving bowls. Place the reserved carrots, celery and cucumber on top of the noodles, arrange the duck slices on top and drizzle with the sauce. Serve immediately.

duck & radish salad

ingredients

SERVES 4

350 g/12 oz boneless duck
    breasts

2 tbsp plain flour

1 egg

2 tbsp water

2 tbsp sesame seeds

3 tbsp sesame oil

1/2 head Chinese leaves,
    shredded

3 celery sticks, sliced finely

8 radishes, trimmed and
    halved

salt and pepper

fresh basil leaves, to garnish

dressing

finely grated rind of 1 lime

2 tbsp lime juice

2 tbsp olive oil

1 tbsp light soy sauce

1 tbsp chopped fresh basil

salt and pepper

method

1 Put each duck breast between sheets of greaseproof paper or clingfilm. Use a meat mallet or rolling pin to beat them out and flatten them slightly.

2 Sprinkle the flour onto a large plate and season with salt and pepper. Beat the egg and water together in a shallow bowl, then sprinkle the sesame seeds on to a separate plate.

3 Dip the duck breasts first into the seasoned flour, then into the egg mixture and finally into the sesame seeds, to coat the duck evenly. Heat the sesame oil in a preheated wok or large frying pan.

4 Fry the duck breasts over a medium heat for about 8 minutes, turning once. To test whether they are cooked, insert a sharp knife into the thickest part – the juices should run clear. Lift them out and drain on kitchen paper.

5 To make the dressing for the salad, whisk together the lime rind and juice, olive oil, soy sauce and chopped basil. Season with a little salt and pepper.

6 Arrange the Chinese leaves, celery and radishes on a serving plate. Slice the duck breasts thinly and place on top of the salad.

7 Drizzle with the dressing and garnish with fresh basil leaves. Serve at once.

melon, chorizo & artichoke salad

ingredients

SERVES 8

12 small globe artichokes
juice of $1/2$ lemon
2 tbsp olive oil
1 small orange-fleshed melon,
    such as cantaloupe
200 g/7 oz chorizo sausage,
    outer casing removed
fresh tarragon or flat-leaf
    parsley sprigs, to garnish

dressing

3 tbsp extra virgin olive oil
1 tbsp red wine vinegar
1 tsp prepared mustard
1 tbsp chopped fresh
    tarragon
salt and pepper

method

1 Using kitchen scissors cut off the outside layer of leaves from the artichokes and snip off the tough tips. Cut into quarters and brush with lemon juice to prevent discoloration.

2 Heat the olive oil in a large, heavy-based frying pan. Add the prepared artichokes and fry, stirring frequently, for 5 minutes, or until the artichoke leaves are golden brown. Remove from the frying pan, transfer to a large serving bowl and leave to cool.

3 Cut the melon in half and scoop out the seeds. Cut the flesh into bite-sized cubes. Add to the cooled artichokes. Cut the chorizo into bite-sized chunks and add to the melon and artichokes.

4 To make the dressing, place all the ingredients in a small bowl and whisk together. Just before serving, pour the dressing over the prepared salad ingredients and toss together. Serve the salad garnished with tarragon or parsley sprigs.

butter bean, onion & herb salad with spicy sausage

ingredients

SERVES 2

1 tbsp sunflower oil

1 small onion, finely sliced

250 g/9 oz canned butter
     beans, drained and rinsed

1 tsp balsamic vinegar

2 chorizo sausages, sliced
     diagonally

1 small tomato, diced

2 tbsp harissa paste

85 g/3 oz mixed herb salad

method

1 Heat the oil in a non-stick frying pan over a medium heat, add the onion and cook, stirring frequently, until softened but not browned. Add the beans and cook for a further minute, then add the vinegar, stirring well. Keep warm.

2 Meanwhile, heat a separate, dry frying pan over a medium heat, add the chorizo slices and cook, turning occasionally, until lightly browned. Remove with a slotted spoon and drain on kitchen paper.

3 Mix the tomato and harissa paste together in a small bowl. Divide the herb salad between 2 plates, spoon over the bean mixture and scatter over the warm chorizo slices. Top with a spoonful of the tomato and harissa mixture and serve immediately.

crispy spinach & bacon

ingredients

SERVES 4

4 tbsp olive oil

4 rashers of streaky bacon,
diced

1 thick slice of white bread,
crusts removed, cut into
cubes

450 g/1 lb fresh spinach,
torn or shredded

method

1 Heat 2 tablespoons of the olive oil over a
high heat in a large frying pan. Add the diced
bacon to the pan and cook for 3–4 minutes, or
until crisp. Remove with a slotted spoon,
draining carefully, and set aside.

2 Toss the cubes of bread in the fat remaining
in the pan over a high heat for about 4 minutes,
or until crisp and golden. Remove the croûtons
with a slotted spoon, draining carefully, and
set them aside.

3 Add the remaining oil to the frying pan and
heat. Toss the spinach in the oil over a high
heat for about 3 minutes, or until it has just
wilted. Turn into a serving bowl and sprinkle
with the bacon and croûtons. Serve immediately.

egg & bacon salad

ingredients

SERVES 4

1 tbsp sunflower or olive oil
6–8 slices streaky bacon,
 diced
55 g/2 oz fresh breadcrumbs
selection of salad leaves, torn
6–8 hard-boiled eggs,
 quartered
12 black olives

dressing

2 tbsp white wine vinegar
5 tbsp extra virgin olive oil
1 tbsp wholegrain mustard
salt and pepper

method

1 Heat the sunflower or olive oil in a frying pan, add the bacon and cook for about 5 minutes until crisp. Remove from the pan.

2 Add the breadcrumbs to the pan and cook over a high heat until crisp and golden. Set aside.

3 Put the salad leaves into a bowl with the eggs and olives and tip in the bacon.

4 To make the dressing, whisk the vinegar, extra virgin olive oil, mustard and salt and pepper together in a bowl and pour over the salad.

5 Toss to mix, sprinkle with the crisp breadcrumbs and serve immediately.

warm mushroom, spinach & pancetta salad

ingredients

SERVES 4

275 g/9³/₄ oz fresh baby
    spinach leaves
2 tbsp olive oil
150 g/5¹/₂ oz pancetta
280 g/10 oz mixed wild
    mushrooms, sliced

dressing

5 tbsp olive oil
1 tbsp balsamic vinegar
1 tsp Dijon mustard
pinch of sugar
salt and pepper

method

1 To make the dressing, place the olive oil, vinegar, mustard, sugar, salt and pepper in a small bowl and whisk together. Rinse the baby spinach under cold running water, then drain and place in a large salad bowl.

2 Heat the oil in a large frying pan. Add the pancetta and fry for 3 minutes. Add the mushrooms and cook for 3–4 minutes, or until tender.

3 Pour the dressing into the frying pan and immediately turn the fried mixture and dressing into the bowl with the spinach. Toss until coated with the dressing and serve immediately.

roast pork & pumpkin salad

ingredients

SERVES 4–6

1 small pumpkin, about
    1.6 kg/3^{1}/$_{2}$ lb

2 red onions, cut into wedges

olive oil

100 g/3^{1}/$_{2}$ oz green beans,
    topped and tailed and cut
    in half

600 g/1 lb 5 oz roast pork,
    any skin or rind removed
    and cut into bite-sized
    chunks

large handful of fresh rocket
    leaves

100 g/3^{1}/$_{2}$ oz feta cheese,
    drained and crumbled

2 tbsp toasted pine kernels

2 tbsp chopped fresh parsley

salt and pepper

dressing

6 tbsp extra virgin olive oil

3 tbsp balsamic vinegar

^{1}/$_{2}$ tsp sugar

^{1}/$_{2}$ tsp Dijon, prepared English
    or wholegrain mustard

salt and pepper

method

1 Preheat the oven to 200°C/400°F/Gas Mark 6.
Cut the pumpkin in half, scoop out the seeds
and fibres and cut the flesh into wedges
about 4 cm/1^{1}/$_{2}$ inches wide. Very lightly rub
the pumpkin and onion wedges with the olive
oil, place in a roasting pan and roast for
25–30 minutes until the pumpkin and onions
are tender but holding their shape.

2 Meanwhile, bring a small pan of salted water
to the boil. Add the green beans and blanch
for 5 minutes, or until tender. Drain well and
cool under cold running water to stop them
cooking further. Drain well and pat dry.

3 Remove the pumpkin and onion wedges from
the oven as soon as they are tender-crisp and
leave to cool completely. When the pumpkin is
cool, peel and cut into bite-sized pieces.

4 To make the dressing, put the oil, vinegar,
sugar, mustard and salt and pepper to taste
into a screw-top jar and shake until blended.

5 To assemble the salad, put the pumpkin,
onions, beans, pork, rocket, feta, pine kernels
and parsley in a large bowl and gently toss
together – be careful not to break up the
pumpkin. Shake the dressing again, pour over
the salad and gently toss. Divide between
individual bowls and serve.

grilled lamb with yogurt & herb dressing

ingredients

SERVES 4

2 tbsp sunflower oil, plus
extra for grilling the lamb

1 tbsp tomato pureé

$^1/_2$ tbsp ground cumin

1 tsp lemon juice

1 garlic clove, crushed

pinch of cayenne pepper

500 g/1 lb 2 oz lamb neck
fillets, trimmed with
excess fat removed

salt and pepper

toasted sesame seeds and
chopped fresh parsley,
to garnish

dressing

2 tbsp fresh lemon juice

1 tsp clear honey

85 g/3 oz Greek yogurt

2 tbsp finely shredded fresh
mint

2 tbsp chopped fresh parsley

1 tbsp finely snipped fresh
chives

salt and pepper

method

1 Mix the 2 tablespoons oil, tomato pureé, cumin, lemon juice, garlic, cayenne and salt and pepper to taste together in a non-metallic bowl. Add the lamb fillets and rub all over with the marinade. Cover the bowl and marinate in the fridge for at least 2 hours, but ideally overnight.

2 Meanwhile, to make the dressing, whisk the lemon juice and honey together until the honey dissolves. Whisk in the yogurt until well blended. Stir in the herbs and add salt and pepper to taste. Cover and chill until required.

3 Remove the lamb from the fridge 15 minutes before you are ready to cook. Heat the grill to its highest setting and lightly brush the grill rack with oil. Grill the lamb fillet, turning it once, for 10 minutes for medium and 12 minutes for well done. Leave the lamb to cool completely, then cover and chill until required.

4 Thinly slice the lamb fillets, then divide between 4 plates. Adjust the seasoning in the dressing, if necessary, then spoon over the lamb slices. Sprinkle with toasted sesame seeds and parsley and serve.

roast beef salad

ingredients

SERVES 4

750 g/1 lb 10 oz beef fillet,
  trimmed of any visible fat
2 tsp Worcestershire sauce
3 tbsp olive oil
400 g/14 oz green beans
100 g/3^1/$_2$ oz small pasta,
  such as orecchiette
2 red onions, finely sliced
1 large head radicchio
50 g/1^3/$_4$ oz green olives,
  stoned
50 g/1^3/$_4$ oz shelled
  hazelnuts, whole
pepper

dressing

1 tsp Dijon mustard
2 tbsp white wine vinegar
5 tbsp olive oil

method

1 Preheat the oven to 220°C/425°F/Gas Mark 7. Rub the beef with pepper to taste and Worcestershire sauce. Heat 2 tablespoons of the oil in a small roasting tin over a high heat, add the beef and sear on all sides. Transfer the dish to the preheated oven and roast for 30 minutes. Remove and leave to cool.

2 Bring a large saucepan of water to the boil, add the beans and cook for 5 minutes, or until just tender. Remove with a slotted spoon and refresh the beans under cold running water. Drain and put into a large bowl.

3 Return the bean cooking water to the boil, add the pasta and cook for 11 minutes, or until tender. Drain, return to the saucepan and toss with the remaining oil.

4 Add the pasta to the beans with the onions, radicchio leaves, olives and hazelnuts, mix gently and transfer to a serving bowl or dish. Arrange some thinly sliced beef on top.

5 Whisk the dressing ingredients together in a separate bowl, then pour over the salad and serve immediately with extra sliced beef.

warm beef niçoise

ingredients

SERVES 4

4 fillet steaks, about 115 g/
    4 oz each, fat discarded
2 tbsp red wine vinegar
2 tbsp orange juice
2 tsp ready-made English
    mustard
2 eggs
175 g/6 oz new potatoes
115 g/4 oz green beans,
    trimmed
175 g/6 oz mixed salad
    leaves, such as baby
    spinach, rocket and
    mizuna
1 yellow pepper, peeled,
    skinned and cut into strips
175 g/6 oz cherry tomatoes,
    halved
black olives, stoned,
    to garnish (optional)
2 tsp extra virgin olive oil

method

1 Place the steaks in a shallow dish. Blend the vinegar with 1 tablespoon of orange juice and 1 teaspoon of mustard. Pour over the steaks, cover and leave in the refrigerator for at least 30 minutes. Turn over halfway through the marinating time.

2 Place the eggs in a pan and cover with cold water. Bring to the boil, then reduce the heat to a simmer and cook for 10 minutes. Remove and plunge the eggs into cold water. Once cold, shell and reserve.

3 Meanwhile, place the potatoes in a saucepan and cover with cold water. Bring to the boil, cover and simmer for 15 minutes, or until tender when pierced with a fork. Drain and reserve.

4 Bring a saucepan of water to the boil, add the beans and cook for 5 minutes, or until just tender. Drain, plunge into cold water and drain again. Arrange the potatoes and beans on top of the salad leaves together with the yellow pepper, cherry tomatoes and olives, if using. Blend the remaining orange juice and mustard with the olive oil and reserve.

5 Heat a griddle pan until smoking. Drain the steaks and cook for 3–5 minutes on each side or according to personal preference. Slice the steaks and arrange on top of the salad, then pour over the dressing and serve.

chilli beef stir-fry salad

ingredients

SERVES 4

450 g/1 lb lean rump steak
2 cloves garlic, crushed
1 tsp chilli powder
$^1/_2$ tsp salt
1 tsp ground coriander
1 ripe avocado
2 tbsp sunflower oil
425 g/15 oz canned red
    kidney beans, drained
175 g/6 oz cherry tomatoes,
    halved
1 large packet tortilla chips
shredded iceberg lettuce
chopped fresh coriander,
    to serve

method

1 Using a sharp knife, slice the beef into thin strips.

2 Place the garlic, chilli powder, salt and ground coriander in a large bowl and mix until well combined.

3 Add the strips of beef to the marinade and toss well to coat all over.

4 Halve, peel and stone the avocados. Slice the avocado lengthways and then crossways to form small cubes.

5 Heat the oil in a large preheated wok. Add the beef and stir-fry for 5 minutes, tossing frequently.

6 Add the kidney beans, tomatoes and avocado and heat through for 2 minutes.

7 Arrange a bed of tortilla chips and iceberg lettuce around the edge of a large serving plate and spoon the beef mixture into the centre. Alternatively, serve the tortilla chips and iceberg lettuce separately.

8 Garnish with chopped fresh coriander and serve immediately.

grilled beef salad

ingredients

SERVES 4

50 g/1¾ oz dried oyster
    mushrooms

600 g/1 lb 5 oz rump steak

1 red pepper, deseeded and
    sliced thinly

40 g/1½ oz roasted cashew
    nuts

red and green lettuce leaves,
    to serve

mint leaves, to garnish

dressing

2 tbsp sesame oil

2 tbsp fish sauce

2 tbsp sweet sherry

2 tbsp oyster sauce

1 tbsp lime juice

1 fresh red chilli, deseeded
    and chopped finely

method

1 Place the mushrooms in a bowl, cover with boiling water and leave to stand for 20 minutes. Drain and cut into thin slices.

2 To make the dressing, place the sesame oil, fish sauce, sherry, oyster sauce, lime juice and chilli in a bowl and whisk to combine.

3 Grill the steak, either on a ridged iron griddle pan or under the grill, turning once, for 5 minutes, or until browned on both sides and rare in the middle, or cook longer if desired.

4 Slice the steak into thin strips and place in a bowl with the mushrooms, pepper and nuts. Add the dressing and toss together.

5 Arrange the lettuce on a large serving platter and place the steak mixture on top. Garnish with mint leaves. Serve at room temperature.

rare roast beef pasta salad

ingredients

SERVES 4

450 g/1 lb rump or sirloin
  steak in a single piece
450 g/1 lb dried fusilli
4 tbsp olive oil
2 tbsp lime juice
2 tbsp fish sauce
2 tsp clear honey
4 spring onions, sliced
1 cucumber, peeled and cut
  into 2.5 cm/1 inch chunks
3 tomatoes, cut into wedges
1 tbsp finely chopped fresh
  mint
salt and pepper

method

1 Season the steak with salt and pepper. Grill or pan-fry it for 4 minutes on each side. Allow to rest for 5 minutes, then slice thinly across the grain.

2 Meanwhile, bring a large saucepan of lightly salted water to the boil. Add the pasta, bring back to the boil and cook for 8–10 minutes or until tender, but still firm to the bite. Drain the fusilli, refresh in cold water and drain again thoroughly. Toss the fusilli in the olive oil and set aside until required.

3 Combine the lime juice, fish sauce and honey in a small saucepan and cook over a medium heat for 2 minutes.

4 Add the spring onions, cucumber, tomatoes and mint to the pan, then add the steak and mix well. Season to taste with salt.

5 Transfer the fusilli to a large, warm serving dish and top with the steak and salad mixture. Serve just warm or allow to cool completely.

beef & peanut salad

ingredients

SERVES 4

1/2 head Chinese leaves

1 large carrot

125 g/4 1/2 oz radishes

100 g/3 1/2 oz baby sweetcorn

1 tbsp groundnut oil

1 red chilli, deseeded and
    chopped finely

1 clove garlic, chopped finely

350 g/12 oz lean beef (such
    as tenderloin, sirloin, or
    top round), trimmed of
    any visible fat and sliced

1 tbsp dark soy sauce

25 g/1 oz fresh peanuts
    (optional)

red chilli, sliced, to garnish

dressing

1 tbsp smooth peanut butter

1 tsp caster sugar

2 tbsp light soy sauce

1 tbsp sherry vinegar

salt and pepper

method

1 Finely shred the Chinese leaves and arrange attractively on a platter.

2 Peel the carrot and cut into very thin strips. Wash, trim, and quarter the radishes, and halve the sweetcorn lengthways. Arrange these ingredients around the edge of the dish and set aside.

3 Heat the groundnut oil in a non-stick wok or large frying pan until really hot.

4 Add the red chilli, garlic and beef to the wok or skillet and cook for 5 minutes.

5 Add the dark soy sauce and cook for a further 1-2 minutes until tender and cooked through.

6 Meanwhile, make the dressing. Place all of the ingredients in a small bowl and blend them together until smooth.

7 Place the hot cooked beef in the centre of the salad ingredients. Spoon over the dressing and sprinkle with a few peanuts, if using. Garnish with slices of red chilli and serve immediately.

fish & seafood salads

Seafood has always been a popular salad ingredient – crab and prawn salads have almost become a cliché, although a very pleasant one. Some varieties of fish, such as fresh or smoked salmon and fresh or canned tuna, are also favourite ingredients and there are others that, although less familiar in salads, are just as tasty. Perhaps this is because the delicate flavour and light texture of fish and seafood combine so well with all kinds of salad ingredients from pasta to fruit and from beans to rocket.

Fish and seafood salads probably offer more scope for variety than any other type because they respond so delightfully to different flavours. Prawns, for example, are as delicious with the Mediterranean flavours of olive oil, lemon juice, olives and tomatoes as they are with the Southeast Asian taste of chillies and tropical fruits. Fresh vegetables and earthy lentils both complement the richness of tuna in very different but equally delicious ways. And, of course, fish and seafood look and taste superb served together in a mixed seafood salad with a fragrant dressing.

Salads are a good way to encourage the family to eat more fish as the flavour, aroma and texture are quite different from and more subtle than those of hot fish dishes which can put some people off. They are also often very colourful, making them especially tempting.

salmon & avocado salad

ingredients

SERVES 4

450 g/1 lb new potatoes

4 salmon steaks, about
115 g/4 oz each

1 avocado

juice of 1/2 lemon

55 g/2 oz baby spinach
leaves

125 g/4 1/2 oz mixed small
salad leaves, including
watercress

12 cherry tomatoes, halved

55 g/2 oz chopped walnuts

dressing

3 tbsp unsweetened clear
apple juice

1 tsp balsamic vinegar

pepper

method

1 Cut the new potatoes into bite-sized pieces, put into a saucepan and cover with cold water. Bring to the boil, then reduce the heat, cover and simmer for 10–15 minutes, or until just tender. Drain and keep warm.

2 Meanwhile, preheat the grill to medium. Cook the salmon steaks under the preheated grill for 10–15 minutes, depending on the thickness of the steaks, turning halfway through cooking. Remove from the grill and keep warm.

3 While the potatoes and salmon are cooking, cut the avocado in half, remove and discard the stone and peel the flesh. Cut the avocado flesh into slices and coat in the lemon juice to prevent it from discolouring.

4 Toss the spinach leaves and mixed salad leaves together in a large serving bowl until combined, then divide between 4 serving plates. Arrange 6 cherry tomato halves on each plate of salad.

5 Remove and discard the skin and any bones from the salmon. Flake the salmon and divide between the plates along with the potatoes. Sprinkle the walnuts over the salads.

6 To make the dressing, mix the apple juice and vinegar together in a small bowl or jug and season well with pepper. Drizzle over the salads and serve immediately.

smoked salmon, asparagus & avocado salad

ingredients

SERVES 4

200 g/7 oz fresh asparagus
    spears
1 large ripe avocado
1 tbsp lemon juice
large handful fresh rocket
    leaves
225 g/8 oz smoked salmon
    slices
1 red onion, finely sliced
1 tbsp fresh flat-leaf parsley,
    chopped
1 tbsp chopped fresh chives

dressing

1 garlic clove, chopped
4 tbsp extra virgin olive oil
2 tbsp white wine vinegar
1 tbsp lemon juice
pinch of sugar
1 tsp mustard

method

1 Bring a large saucepan of lightly salted water to the boil. Add the asparagus and cook for 4 minutes, then drain. Refresh under cold running water and drain again. Set aside to cool.

2 To make the dressing, combine all the ingredients in a small bowl and stir together well. Cut the avocado in half lengthways, then remove and discard the stone and skin. Cut the flesh into bite-sized pieces and brush with lemon juice to prevent discoloration.

3 To assemble the salad, arrange the rocket leaves on individual serving plates and top with the asparagus and avocado. Cut the smoked salmon into strips and scatter over the top of the salad, then scatter over the onion and herbs. Drizzle over the dressing and serve.

tomato, salmon & prawn salad

ingredients

SERVES 4

several lettuce leaves

115 g/4 oz cherry tomatoes, halved

4 ripe tomatoes, roughly chopped

100 g/3^1/$_2$ oz smoked salmon

200 g/7 oz large cooked prawns, thawed if frozen

dressing

1 tbsp Dijon mustard

2 tsp caster sugar

2 tsp red wine vinegar

2 tbsp medium olive oil

few fresh dill sprigs, plus extra to garnish

pepper

method

1 Place the lettuce leaves around the edge of a shallow bowl and add the cherry tomatoes. Using the lettuce leaves around the edge of a shallow bowl and add all the tomatoes and cherry tomatoes. Using scissors, snip the smoked salmon into strips and scatter over the tomatoes, then add the prawns.

2 Mix the mustard, sugar, vinegar and oil together in a small bowl, then tear most of the dill sprigs into it. Mix well and pour over the salad. Toss well to coat the salad with the dressing. Snip the remaining dill over the top and season to taste with pepper.

tuna & herbed fusilli salad

ingredients

SERVES 4

200 g/7 oz dried fusilli

1 red pepper, deseeded and
    quartered

1 red onion, sliced

4 tomatoes, sliced

200 g/7 oz canned tuna in
    brine, drained and flaked

dressing

6 tbsp basil-flavoured oil or
    extra virgin olive oil

3 tbsp white wine vinegar

1 tbsp lime juice

1 tsp mustard

1 tsp honey

4 tbsp chopped fresh basil,
    plus extra sprigs to garnish

method

1 Bring a large saucepan of lightly salted water to the boil. Add the pasta, return to the boil and cook for 8–10 minutes until tender but still firm to the bite.

2 Meanwhile, put the pepper quarters under a preheated hot grill and cook for 10–12 minutes until the skins begin to blacken. Transfer to a polythene bag, seal and set aside.

3 Remove the pasta from the heat, drain and set aside to cool. Remove the pepper quarters from the bag and peel off the skins. Slice the pepper into strips.

4 To make the dressing, put all the dressing ingredients in a large bowl and stir together well. Add the pasta, pepper strips, onion, tomatoes and tuna. Toss together gently, then divide between serving bowls. Garnish with basil sprigs and serve.

tuna & fresh vegetable salad

ingredients

SERVES 4

12 cherry tomatoes, halved

225 g/8 oz whole green beans,
   cut into 2.5 cm/1 inch
   pieces

225 g/8 oz courgettes, sliced
   thinly

225 g/8 oz button mushrooms,
   sliced thinly

salad leaves

350 g/12 oz canned tuna in
   brine, drained and flaked

fresh parsley, to garnish

dressing

4 tbsp mayonnaise

4 tbsp natural yogurt

2 tbsp white wine vinegar

salt and pepper

method

1 To make the dressing, put the mayonnaise, yogurt, vinegar, salt and pepper to taste in a screw-top jar and shake together until the ingredients are well blended.

2 Put the cherry tomatoes, beans, courgettes and mushrooms in a bowl. Pour over the dressing and leave to marinate for about 1 hour.

3 Arrange the salad leaves on a serving dish. Add the vegetables and then the tuna and garnish with parsley.

lentil & tuna salad

ingredients

SERVES 4

2 ripe tomatoes

1 small red onion

400 g/14 oz canned lentils,
    drained

185 g/6^1/$_2$ oz canned tuna,
    drained

2 tbsp chopped fresh
    coriander

pepper

dressing

3 tbsp virgin olive oil

1 tbsp lemon juice

1 tsp wholegrain mustard

1 garlic clove, crushed

^{1}/$_2$ tsp ground cumin

^{1}/$_2$ tsp ground coriander

method

1 Using a sharp knife, deseed the tomatoes and then chop them into small cubes. Finely chop the red onion.

2 To make the dressing, whisk together the virgin olive oil, lemon juice, mustard, garlic, cumin and ground coriander in a small bowl until thoroughly combined. Set aside until required.

3 Mix together the chopped onion, diced tomatoes and drained lentils in a large bowl.

4 Flake the tuna with a fork and stir it into the onion, tomato and lentil mixture. Stir in the chopped fresh coriander and mix well.

5 Pour the dressing over the lentil and tuna salad and season with pepper to taste. Serve immediately.

tuna & two-bean salad

ingredients

SERVES 4

200 g/7 oz green beans

400 g/14 oz canned small
    white beans, such as
    cannellini, rinsed and
    drained

4 spring onions, finely
    chopped

2 fresh tuna steaks, about
    225 g/8 oz each and
    2 cm/³/4 inch thick

olive oil, for brushing

250 g/9 oz cherry tomatoes,
    halved

lettuce leaves

salt and pepper

fresh mint and parsley sprigs,
    to garnish

dressing

handful of fresh mint leaves,
    shredded

handful of fresh parsley
    leaves, chopped

1 garlic clove, crushed

4 tbsp extra virgin olive oil

1 tbsp red wine vinegar

salt and pepper

method

1 First, make the dressing. Put the mint leaves, parsley leaves, garlic, olive oil and vinegar into a screw-top jar, add salt and pepper to taste and shake until blended. Pour into a large bowl and set aside.

2 Bring a saucepan of lightly salted water to the boil. Add the green beans and cook for 3 minutes. Add the white beans and cook for a further 4 minutes until the green beans are tender-crisp and the white beans are heated through. Drain well and add to the bowl with the dressing and spring onions. Toss together.

3 To cook the tuna, heat a ridged griddle pan over a high heat. Lightly brush the tuna steaks with oil, then season to taste with salt and pepper. Cook the steaks for 2 minutes, then turn over and cook on the other side for a further 2 minutes for rare or up to 4 minutes for well done.

4 Remove the tuna from the griddle pan and leave to rest for 2 minutes, or alternatively leave until completely cool. When ready to serve, add the tomatoes to the bean mixture and toss lightly. Line a serving platter with lettuce leaves and pile on the bean salad. Place the tuna over the top. Serve warm or at room temperature, garnished with the herbs.

sweet & sour fish salad

ingredients

SERVES 4

225 g/8 oz trout fillets

225 g/8 oz white fish fillets
(such as haddock or cod)

300 ml/10 fl oz water

1 stalk lemon grass

2 lime leaves

1 large red chilli

1 bunch spring onions,
trimmed and shredded

115 g/4 oz fresh pineapple
flesh

1 small red pepper, deseeded
and diced

1 bunch watercress, washed
and trimmed

fresh snipped chives,
to garnish

dressing

1 tbsp sunflower oil

1 tbsp rice wine vinegar

pinch of chilli powder

1 tsp clear honey

salt and pepper

method

1 Rinse the fish, place in a frying pan and pour over the water. Bend the lemon grass in half to bruise it and add to the pan with the lime leaves. Prick the chilli with a fork and add to the pan. Bring to the boil and simmer for 7–8 minutes. Let cool.

2 Drain the fish fillet thoroughly, flake the flesh away from the skin and place in a bowl. Gently stir in the spring onions, pineapple and pepper.

3 Arrange the washed watercress on 4 serving plates and spoon the cooked fish mixture on top.

4 To make the dressing, mix all the ingredients together, seasoning well. Spoon over the fish and serve garnished with chives.

smoked trout with pears

ingredients

SERVES 4

55 g/2 oz watercress

1 head of radicchio, torn into
pieces

4 smoked trout fillets, skinned

2 ripe pears, such as Williams

2 tbsp lemon juice

2 tbsp extra virgin olive oil

3 tbsp soured cream

2 tsp creamed horseradish

salt and pepper

thinly sliced buttered brown
bread, crusts removed,
to serve

method

1 Place the watercress and radicchio in a bowl. Cut the trout fillets into thin strips and add to the bowl. Halve and core the pears, then slice thinly. Place in a separate bowl, add 4 teaspoons of the lemon juice and toss to coat. Add the pears to the salad.

2 To make the dressing, mix the remaining lemon juice and the olive oil together in a bowl, then season to taste with salt and pepper. Pour the dressing over the salad and toss well. Transfer to a large salad bowl.

3 Mix the soured cream and horseradish together in a separate bowl until thoroughly blended, then serve with the salad, together with the buttered bread.

skate & spinach salad

ingredients

SERVES 4

700 g/1 lb 9 oz skate wings,
    trimmed

2 fresh rosemary sprigs

1 fresh bay leaf

1 tbsp black peppercorns

1 lemon, quartered

450 g/1 lb baby spinach
    leaves

1 tbsp olive oil

1 small red onion, thinly sliced

2 garlic cloves, crushed

1/2 tsp chilli flakes

50 g/1 3/4 oz pine kernels,
    lightly toasted

50 g/1 3/4 oz raisins

1 tbsp light muscovado sugar

2 tbsp chopped fresh parsley

method

1 Put the skate into a large saucepan with the herbs, peppercorns and lemon. Cover with water and bring to the boil. Cover and simmer for 4–5 minutes until the flesh begins to come away from the cartilage. Remove from the heat and set aside for 15 minutes. Lift the fish from the water and remove the flesh in shreds.

2 Meanwhile, put the spinach into a pan with just the water that clings to the leaves after washing. Cook over a high heat for 30 seconds until wilted. Drain, refresh under cold water and drain again. Squeeze out any excess water and set aside.

3 Heat the oil in a large frying pan. Fry the onion for 3–4 minutes until softened, but not browned. Add the garlic, chilli flakes, pine kernels, raisins and sugar. Cook for 1–2 minutes, then add the spinach and toss for 1 minute until heated through. Gently fold in the skate and cook for a further minute. Season well.

4 Divide the salad between 4 serving plates and sprinkle with the parsley.

anchovies with celery & rocket

ingredients

SERVES 4

2 celery sticks, strings
    removed

4 small handfuls of rocket

12–16 brine-cured anchovy
    fillets, halved lengthways

1$^1/_2$ tbsp extra virgin olive oil

salt and pepper

thick lemon wedges, to serve

method

1 Quarter the celery sticks lengthways and slice into 7.5-cm/3-inch batons. Soak in ice-cold water for 30 minutes, until crisp and slightly curled, then drain and pat dry.

2 Place a small pile of rocket on individual serving plates. Arrange the celery and anchovy fillets attractively on top. Spoon over a little olive oil and season with salt and pepper, bearing in mind the saltiness of the anchovies. Serve with thick wedges of lemon.

anchovy & olive salad

ingredients

SERVES 4

large handful of mixed lettuce
    leaves
12 cherry tomatoes, halved
20 black olives, stoned and
    halved
6 canned anchovy fillets,
    drained and thinly sliced
1 tbsp chopped fresh oregano
wedges of lemon, to garnish
crusty bread rolls, to serve

dressing

4 tbsp extra virgin olive oil
1 tbsp white wine vinegar
1 tbsp lemon juice
1 tbsp chopped fresh flat-leaf
    parsley
salt and pepper

method

1 To make the dressing, put all the ingredients into a small bowl, season with salt and pepper and stir together well.

2 To assemble the salad, arrange the lettuce leaves in a serving dish. Scatter the cherry tomatoes on top, followed by the olives, anchovies and oregano. Drizzle over the dressing.

3 Transfer to individual plates, garnish with lemon wedges, and serve with crusty bread rolls.

celeriac rémoulade with crab

ingredients

SERVES 4

450 g/1 lb celeriac, peeled
and grated
juice of 1 lemon
250 g/9 oz fresh white
crabmeat, picked over
chopped fresh dill or parsley,
to garnish

rémoulade
dressing

150 ml/5 fl oz mayonnaise
1 tbsp Dijon mustard
1$\frac{1}{2}$ tsp white wine vinegar
2 tbsp capers in brine,
well rinsed
salt and white pepper

method

1 To make the dressing, put the mayonnaise in a bowl. Beat in the mustard, vinegar and capers with salt and white pepper to taste – the mixture should be piquant with a strong mustard flavour. Cover and chill until required.

2 Bring a large pan of salted water to a full, rolling boil. Meanwhile, peel the celeriac and cut it into quarters, then grate it either in a food processor or on the coarse side of a box grater.

3 Add the grated celeriac and lemon juice to the water and blanch for 1$\frac{1}{2}$–2 minutes until it is just slightly tender. Rinse the celeriac well, then put it under cold running water to stop the cooking. Use your hands to squeeze out the excess moisture, then pat the celeriac dry with kitchen paper or a clean tea towel.

4 Stir the celeriac into the dressing, along with the crabmeat. Taste and adjust the seasoning, if necessary. Cover and chill for at least 30 minutes.

5 When ready to serve, spoon into bowls and sprinkle with dill or parsley.

cantaloupe & crab salad

ingredients

SERVES 4

350 g/12 oz fresh crabmeat

5 tbsp mayonnaise

50 ml/2 fl oz natural yogurt

4 tsp extra virgin olive oil

4 tsp lime juice

1 spring onion, finely chopped

4 tsp finely chopped fresh
    parsley

pinch of cayenne pepper

1 cantaloupe melon

2 radicchio heads, separated
    into leaves

fresh parsley sprigs,
    to garnish

crusty bread, to serve

method

1 Place the crabmeat in a large bowl and pick over it very carefully to remove any remaining shell or cartilage, but try not to break the meat up.

2 Place the mayonnaise, yogurt, olive oil, lime juice, spring onion, chopped fresh parsley and cayenne pepper into a separate bowl and mix until thoroughly blended. Fold in the crabmeat.

3 Cut the melon in half and scoop out the seeds. Slice into wedges, then cut off the rind with a sharp knife.

4 Arrange the melon wedges and radicchio leaves in 4 serving bowls, then arrange the crabmeat mixture on top. Garnish with a few sprigs of fresh parsley and serve with crusty bread.

chilli prawns with pineapple & papaya salsa

ingredients

SERVES 8

4 tbsp sunflower oil

1 fresh red chilli, deseeded
and chopped

1 garlic clove, crushed

48 prawns

chopped fresh parsley,
to garnish

pineapple & papaya salsa

1 large papaya, halved,
deseeded, peeled, and cut
into 5-mm/$\frac{1}{4}$-inch dice

1 small pineapple, halved,
cored, peeled, and cut
into 5-mm/$\frac{1}{4}$-inch dice

2 spring onions, very finely
chopped

1 red chilli, or to taste,
deseeded and finely
chopped

1 garlic clove, very finely
chopped

2$\frac{1}{2}$ tsp lemon juice

$\frac{1}{2}$ tsp ground cumin

$\frac{1}{4}$ tsp salt

black pepper

method

1 To make the salsa, put the papaya in a large bowl with the pineapple, spring onions, chilli, garlic, lemon juice, cumin, salt and pepper. Adjust the lemon juice, cumin, salt or pepper to taste, if necessary. Cover and chill until required, ideally at least 2 hours.

2 Heat a wok over a high heat. Add the oil and swirl around, then add the chilli and garlic and stir-fry for 20 seconds. Add the prawns and stir-fry for 2–3 minutes until the prawns are cooked through, become pink and curl.

3 Tip the prawns, garlic and any oil left in the wok into a heatproof bowl and leave the prawns to cool and marinate in the chilli oil. When the prawns are completely cool, cover the bowl and chill for at least 2 hours.

4 When ready to serve, give the salsa a stir and adjust the seasoning, if necessary. Arrange a mound of salsa on each of 8 plates. Remove the prawns from the marinade and divide between plates. Sprinkle with parsley and serve.

prawn & rice salad

ingredients

SERVES 4

175 g/6 oz mixed long-grain
    and wild rice
350 g/12 oz cooked, peeled
    prawns
1 mango, peeled, stoned and
    diced
4 spring onions, sliced
25 g/1 oz flaked almonds
1 tbsp finely chopped fresh
    mint
salt and pepper

dressing

1 tbsp extra virgin olive oil
2 tsp lime juice
1 garlic clove, crushed
1 tsp clear honey
salt and pepper

method

1 Cook the rice in a large saucepan of lightly salted boiling water for 35 minutes, or until tender. Drain and transfer to a large bowl, then add the prawns.

2 To make the dressing, mix all the ingredients together in a large jug, seasoning to taste with the salt and pepper, and whisk well until thoroughly blended. Pour the dressing over the rice and prawn mixture and leave to cool.

3 Add the mango, spring onions, almonds and mint to the salad and season to taste with pepper. Stir thoroughly, transfer to a large serving dish and serve.

chilli squid with watercress & baby spinach salad

ingredients

SERVES 4

12 squid tubes and tentacles (about 700 g/1 lb 9 oz total weight), cleaned and prepared

2–3 tbsp olive oil

1–2 red chillies, deseeded and thinly sliced

2 spring onions, finely chopped

lemon wedges, for squeezing and to serve

3 good handfuls watercress

2 handfuls baby spinach

salt and pepper

dressing

100 ml/3^{1}/$_{2}$ fl oz olive oil

juice of 1 lime

1 tsp caster sugar

2 shallots, thinly sliced

1 tomato, peeled, deseeded and finely chopped

1 garlic clove, crushed

method

1 To make the dressing, mix all the ingredients together in a bowl, season with salt and pepper to taste, cover and refrigerate until required.

2 Cut the squid tubes into 5-cm/2-inch pieces, then score diamond patterns lightly across the flesh with the tip of a sharp knife. Heat the oil in a wok or large frying pan over a high heat, add the squid pieces and tentacles and stir-fry for 1 minute. Add the chillies and spring onions and stir-fry for a further minute. Season to taste with salt and pepper and add a good squeeze of lemon juice.

3 Mix the watercress and spinach together, then toss with enough of the dressing to coat lightly. Serve immediately with the squid, together with lemon wedges to squeeze over the squid.

coconut prawns with cucumber salad

ingredients

SERVES 4

200 g/7 oz brown basmati rice

1/2 tsp coriander seeds

2 egg whites, lightly beaten

100 g/3 1/2 oz unsweetened desiccated coconut

24 raw tiger prawns, peeled

1/2 cucumber

4 spring onions, thinly sliced lengthways

1 tsp sesame oil

1 tbsp finely chopped fresh coriander

method

1 Bring a large saucepan of water to the boil, add the rice and cook for 25 minutes, or until tender. Drain and keep in a colander covered with a clean tea towel to absorb the steam.

2 Meanwhile, soak 8 wooden skewers in cold water for 30 minutes, then drain. Crush the coriander seeds in a mortar with a pestle. Heat a non-stick frying pan over a medium heat, add the crushed coriander seeds and cook, turning, until they begin to colour. Tip onto a plate and set aside.

3 Put the egg whites into a shallow bowl and the coconut into a separate bowl. Roll each prawn first in the egg whites, then in the coconut. Thread onto a skewer. Repeat so that each skewer is threaded with 3 coated prawns.

4 Preheat the grill to high. Using a potato peeler, peel long strips from the cucumber to create ribbons, put into a colander to drain, then toss with the spring onions and oil in a bowl and set aside.

5 Cook the prawns under the preheated grill for 3–4 minutes on each side, or until slightly browned.

6 Meanwhile, mix the rice with the toasted coriander seeds and fresh coriander and divide this and the cucumber salad between bowls. Serve with the hot prawn skewers.

prawn & mango salad

ingredients

SERVES 4

2 mangoes (reserve the juice
    for the dressing)
225 g/8 oz peeled, cooked
    prawns
salad leaves, to serve
4 whole cooked prawns,
    to garnish

dressing

6 tbsp natural yogurt
2 tbsp mayonnaise
1 tbsp lemon juice
salt and pepper

method

1 Cutting close to the stone, cut a large slice from one side of each mango, then cut another slice from the opposite side. Without breaking the skin, cut the flesh in the segments into squares, then push the skin inside out to expose the cubes and cut away from the skin. Use a sharp knife to peel the remaining centre section and cut the flesh away from the stone into cubes. Reserve any juice in a bowl and put the mango flesh in a separate bowl.

2 Add the prawns to the mango flesh. To the juice, add the yogurt, mayonnaise, lemon juice, salt and pepper and blend together.

3 Arrange the salad leaves on a serving dish and add the mango flesh and prawns. Pour over the dressing and serve garnished with the whole prawns.

ceviche

ingredients

SERVES 4

8 fresh scallops

16 large prawns in shells

2 sea bass fillets, about
150 g/5¹/2 oz each, skinned

1 large lemon

1 lime

1 red onion, thinly sliced

¹/2 fresh red chilli, deseeded
and finely chopped

2–4 tbsp extra virgin olive oil

to serve

salad leaves

lemon or lime wedges

pepper

method

1 If the scallops are in shells, use an oyster knife or small knife to prise the shells open, then rinse under running cold water. Cut the scallops and coral free from the shells. Slice the scallop flesh into 2–3 horizontal slices each. Place in a non-metallic bowl with the corals.

2 Remove the heads of, and peel, the prawns. Using a small sharp knife, devein them. Add to the scallops.

3 Cut the sea bass fillet into thin slices across the grain and add to the bowl of seafood.

4 Firmly roll the lemon and lime backwards and forwards on a work surface to help release the juice. Cut the lemon in half and squeeze the juice over the fish. Repeat with the lime.

5 Gently stir to coat the seafood well in the citrus juices, then cover with clingfilm and chill in the refrigerator for 2 hours or until the seafood becomes opaque, but do not leave for longer otherwise the seafood will be too soft.

6 Using a slotted spoon, transfer the seafood to another bowl. Add the onion, chilli and olive oil and stir gently. Set aside at room temperature for about 5 minutes.

7 Spoon the seafood on to individual serving plates and serve immediately with salad leaves, lemon or lime wedges and black pepper.

mixed seafood salad

ingredients

SERVES 4–6

2 garlic cloves, crushed

juice of 1¹/₂ lemons

4 tbsp extra virgin olive oil

2 tbsp chopped fresh flat-leaf
parsley

600 g/1 lb 5 oz cooked
seafood cocktail (prawns,
mussels, clams, calamari
rings, cockles)

1 roasted red pepper, sliced
into thin strips

12 black olives, pitted

2 tbsp shredded fresh basil

salt and pepper

method

1 Whisk the garlic, lemon juice, olive oil and parsley with salt and pepper to taste.

2 Drain the seafood if necessary, and tip into a serving dish. Add the red pepper and olives, then mix with the garlic mixture, turning to coat. Leave in a cool place for 30 minutes to allow the flavours to develop.

3 Stir again before serving, check the seasoning and sprinkle with the basil.

seafood & spinach salad

ingredients

SERVES 4

500 g/1 lb 2 oz live mussels,
 soaked and cleaned
100 g/3^{1}/$_{2}$ oz prawns, peeled
 and deveined
350 g/12 oz scallops
500 g/1 lb 2 oz baby spinach
 leaves
3 spring onions, finely sliced

dressing

4 tbsp extra virgin olive oil
2 tbsp white wine vinegar
1 tbsp lemon juice
1 tsp finely grated lemon rind
1 garlic clove, chopped
1 tbsp grated fresh ginger
1 small red chilli, deseeded
 and diced
1 tbsp chopped fresh
 coriander
salt and pepper

method

1 Put the mussels into a large pan with a little water, bring to the boil and cook over a high heat for 4 minutes. Drain and reserve the liquid. Discard any mussels that remain closed. Return the reserved liquid to the pan and bring to the boil. Add the prawns and scallops and cook for 3 minutes. Drain. Remove the mussels from their shells. Rinse the mussels, prawns and scallops in cold water, drain and put them in a large bowl. Cool, cover with clingfilm and chill for 45 minutes.

2 Meanwhile, rinse the baby spinach leaves and transfer them to a pan with 4 tablespoons of water. Cook over a high heat for 1 minute, transfer to a colander, refresh under cold running water and drain.

3 To make the dressing, put all the ingredients into a small bowl and mix.

4 Arrange the spinach on serving dishes, then scatter over half of the spring onions. Top with the mussels, prawns and scallops, then scatter over the remaining spring onions. Drizzle over the dressing and serve.

mussel salad

ingredients

SERVES 4

2 large red peppers,
    deseeded and halved

350 g/12 oz cooked, shelled
    mussels, thawed if frozen

1 head radicchio

25 g/1 oz rocket

8 cooked green-lipped
    mussels in their shells

dressing

1 tbsp olive oil

1 tbsp lemon juice

1 tsp finely grated lemon rind

2 tsp clear honey

1 tsp French mustard

1 tbsp snipped fresh chives

salt and pepper

method

1 Put the peppers, skin-side up, on the grill rack and grill under a preheated hot grill for 8–10 minutes, or until the skin is charred and blistered and the flesh is soft. Remove from the rack with tongs, put into a bowl and cover with clingfilm. Leave for about 10 minutes, or until cool enough to handle, then peel off the skins.

2 Slice the pepper flesh into thin strips and put into a bowl. Gently stir in the shelled mussels.

3 To make the dressing, whisk the oil, lemon juice and rind, honey, mustard and chives together in a bowl until well blended. Season to taste with salt and pepper. Add the pepper and mussel mixture and toss gently until well coated.

4 Remove the central core of the radicchio and shred the leaves. Put into a serving bowl with the rocket and toss together.

5 Pile the mussel mixture into the centre of the leaves and arrange the green-lipped mussels in their shells around the edge of the bowl.

octopus with lemon & chilli dressing

ingredients

SERVES 4

2 kg/4 lb 8 oz octopus,
    cleaned and gutted

350–425 ml/12–15 fl oz olive
    oil

juice and finely grated rind of
    1 lemon

1–2 green chillies, deseeded
    and finely chopped

1–2 garlic cloves, finely
    chopped

1 tbsp chopped fresh
    coriander

salt and pepper

salad leaves, to serve

method

1 Preheat the oven to 150°C/300°F/Gas Mark 2.

2 Place the octopus in a lidded casserole just large enough to hold it and pour in just enough olive oil to cover. Cover and cook in the preheated oven for 2 hours, until very tender.

3 Drain the octopus well and discard the cooking oil. Separate the tentacles and run your hand firmly along each one to remove the suckers. Thinly slice the tentacles and place in a bowl.

4 Mix together 125 ml/4 fl oz of the remaining olive oil, the lemon juice and rind, chillies, garlic and coriander in jug. Season to taste with salt and pepper and pour the dressing over the octopus. Toss gently, then cover with clingfilm and chill in the refrigerator for at least 2 hours. Serve on a bed of salad leaves.

dressings, oils & vinegars

Salad dressings are not a last-minute afterthought but an essential part of the whole dish. Freshly made dressings are always tastier than any bottle you can buy at the supermarket and you can adjust the proportions – important from the health point of view, the amount of salt – to suit you. You will be aware from the recipes in the previous chapters that dressings, are intended to complement and enhance the flavours of the salad ingredients not to smother and overpower them and no single dressing will be satisfactory for every kind of salad. However, there are some, such as flavoured vinaigrettes, that work well with many different salads and these form a useful addition to your repertoire.

An easy and delightful way of enhancing salad dressings and giving them a personal touch is to use flavoured oils and vinegars. You can pay quite a lot of money if you buy these in the supermarket or delicatessen but they are actually astonishingly easy and economical to make at home and will keep well in a cool, dark place. Herb oils can be used for cooking as well as salad dressings and spiced vinegars add a real gourmet touch to many meals.

tomato dressing

ingredients

SERVES 2–4

2 tbsp balsamic vinegar, or
red or white wine vinegar

4–6 tbsp extra virgin olive oil

1 tsp Dijon mustard

pinch of caster sugar

1 tbsp torn fresh basil leaves

1 tbsp chopped sun-dried
tomatoes

salt and pepper

method

1 Place all the ingredients in a screw-top jar, secure the top and shake well. Alternatively, beat all the ingredients together in a small bowl. Use as much oil as you like.

2 If you have just salad leaves to dress, 4 tablespoons of oil will be sufficient, but if you have heavier ingredients, such as potatoes, you will need about 6 tablespoons of oil.

3 Use the dressing at once. If you want to store it, do not add the herbs – it will then keep for 3–4 days in the refrigerator.

sweet & sour dressing

ingredients

SERVES 2–4

2 tbsp lemon juice, or red or
    white wine vinegar

4–6 tbsp extra virgin olive oil

1 tsp Dijon mustard

pinch of caster sugar

1 tbsp honey

1 tsp finely grated fresh ginger

1 tbsp toasted sesame seeds

1 tbsp freshly chopped
    parsley

salt and pepper

method

1 Place all the ingredients in a screw-top jar, secure the top and shake well. Alternatively, beat all the ingredients together in a small bowl. Use as much oil as you like.

2 A dressing for salad leaves will require 4 tablespoons of oil, but heavier ingredients, such as potatoes, will require about 6 tablespoons of oil.

green dressing

ingredients

SERVES 4

300 ml/10 fl oz low-fat natural
    yogurt

2 tsp Dijon mustard

2–3 tbsp white wine vinegar

4 tsp sunflower oil

2 tbsp coarsely chopped
    fresh parsley

2 tbsp snipped fresh chives

2 tbsp coarsely chopped
    fresh tarragon

1 spring onion, coarsely
    chopped

1 tbsp coarsely chopped
    watercress

salt and pepper

method

1 Put the yogurt, mustard, vinegar and oil into a food processor and season to taste with salt and pepper. Process on medium speed until thoroughly combined. Add the parsley, chives, tarragon, spring onion and watercress and process for a few seconds to chop finely and blend.

slim-line dressing

ingredients

SERVES 4

300 ml/10 fl oz low-fat natural
    yogurt

1 tsp English mustard

2–3 tbsp lemon juice

4 tsp sunflower oil

salt and pepper

method

1 Put all the ingredients into a food processor, season to taste with salt and pepper and process on medium speed until thoroughly combined.

garlic vinaigrette

ingredients

SERVES 2–4

125 ml/4 fl oz garlic-flavoured
    olive oil

3 tbsp white wine vinegar or
    lemon juice

1–2 garlic cloves, crushed

1 tsp Dijon mustard

1/2 tsp caster sugar

salt and pepper

method

1 Put all the ingredients in a screw-top jar, secure the lid and shake vigorously until an emulsion forms. Taste and adjust the seasoning if necessary.

2 Use at once or store in an airtight container in the refrigerator for up to a month. Remove the garlic cloves after 1 week. Always whisk or shake the dressing before using.

herb vinaigrette

ingredients

SERVES 2–4

125 ml/4 fl oz olive or other
    vegetable oil

3 tbsp white wine vinegar or
    lemon juice

1$\frac{1}{2}$ tbsp chopped fresh
    herbs, such as chives,
    parsley or mint

1 tsp Dijon mustard

$\frac{1}{2}$ tsp caster sugar

salt and pepper

method

1 Put all the ingredients in a screw-top jar, secure the lid, and shake vigorously until a thick emulsion forms. Taste and adjust the seasoning if necessary.

2 Use immediately or store in an airtight container in the refrigerator for up to 3 days. Always whisk or shake the dressing before using, and strain through a fine non-metallic strainer if the herbs begin to darken.

basil oil

ingredients

SERVES 2–4

25g/1 oz fresh basil leaves

2 garlic cloves, halved

250 ml/9 fl oz olive oil

method

1 Wash the basil leaves and dry them well. Prepare a bowl of iced water.

2 Bring a saucepan of water to the boil, add the basil leaves and blanch for 5 seconds. Scoop out the leaves and plunge immediately into the iced water to stop the cooking process. Drain out all the water and squeeze the leaves to get rid of as much of the water as possible. Dry them between layers of kitchen paper. Chop roughly and place in a clean jar. Add the garlic.

3 Gently heat the oil over a low heat until warmed and fragrant – about 5 minutes. Make sure it does not boil or burn. Remove from the heat and pour the oil into a clean jar over the basil leaves. Leave to cool, cover and store in the refrigerator. Strain out the basil within a week.

roasted tomato oil

ingredients

SERVES 2–4

4–6 plum tomatoes

250 ml/9 fl oz rapeseed oil

method

1 Preheat the oven to 200°C/400°F/Gas Mark 6.

2 Thinly slice the tomatoes and place them on a lightly greased baking sheet. Place in the oven and roast until they start to char. Remove from the oven and leave to cool.

3 Heat the oil in a saucepan. Bring almost to the boil and allow to simmer for 1–2 minutes.

4 Combine the tomatoes with the warmed oil, and process in a blender or food processor. Process until the tomatoes are well incorporated into the oil. Strain through muslin and pour into a clean jar. Refrigerate.

rosemary, lemon & thyme oil

ingredients

SERVES 2–4

5 sprigs rosemary (each about 13 cm/5 inches long)

10 to 15 sprigs thyme (each about 13 cm/5 inches long)

zest of 2 lemons

250 ml/9 fl oz rapeseed oil

method

1 Preheat the oven to 150°C/300°F/Gas Mark 2.

2 Remove the leaves from the rosemary and thyme sprigs. Cut the lemon zest into strips.

3 Pour the oil into an ovenproof glass dish and add the leaves and lemon zest strips. Place the dish in the centre of the oven and heat for 1^1/$_2$–2 hours.

4 If you have a digital thermometer, test the oil. It should reach a temperature of 120°C/250°F before you remove it from the oven. Leave to cool for at least 30 minutes.

5 Store the oil in the refrigerator as it is, or strain through muslin and refrigerate.

parsley & coriander oil

ingredients

SERVES 2–4

10 g/^{1}/$_4$ oz fresh parsley
   leaves

10 g/^{1}/$_4$ oz fresh coriander
   leaves

250 ml/9 fl oz rapeseed oil

method

1 Wash and drain the leaves. Prepare a pot of water, bring to the boil and submerge the leaves. Blanch for 5 seconds. Drain the leaves and dry well.

2 Heat the oil in a saucepan, bring almost to the boil and allow to simmer for 1–2 minutes.

3 Combine the warmed oil and leaves in a blender bowl or food processor. Process until well combined.

4 Pour through muslin and strain into a clean jar. Cover and refrigerate.

dill & peppercorn vinegar

ingredients

SERVES 2–4

6 sprigs fresh dill

250 ml/9fl oz cider vinegar

1 tsp whole black
   peppercorns

method

1 Wash and dry the dill.

2 In a saucepan over a medium heat, bring the vinegar to the boil. Lower the heat and simmer for 2 minutes. Add the dill and peppercorns, turn off the heat and leave for several minutes until cooled.

3 Pour into a clean jar, seal and keep in a dark place until ready to use or refrigerate.

lemongrass, ginger & garlic vinegar

ingredients

SERVES 2–4

2 stalks lemon grass

3 garlic cloves, peeled

1 tbsp grated ginger

250 ml/9 fl oz rice wine
    vinegar

method

1 Wash and dry the lower portion of the lemon grass stalks, then crush or bruise them slightly. Cut them if you would like smaller pieces in the jar. Cut the garlic cloves in half lengthways.

2 Place the lemon grass, garlic and ginger in a clean jar.

3 In a saucepan over a medium heat, heat the rice wine vinegar until it starts to bubble around the edges of the pan. Remove from the heat, cool a little, then add to the jar with the other ingredients. When completely cool, cover the jar and store in a dark, dry place.

rosemary & garlic balsamic vinegar

ingredients

SERVES 2–4

ten 5-cm/2-inch sprigs
   rosemary
4 garlic cloves
250 ml/9 fl oz balsamic
   vinegar

method

1 Wash the rosemary sprigs, dry and tear off the leaves from the stems. Split the garlic cloves in half lengthways. Combine the leaves and garlic halves in a clean jar.

2 In a saucepan over a medium heat, heat the balsamic vinegar until it just starts to bubble around the edges of the pan. Wait until it cools a little, then pour into the jar with the rosemary and garlic. When it is completely cool, cover the jar and store in a cool, dark place. Check occasionally to see whether the vinegar has reached the desired strength.

3 Before using, strain the vinegar through a fine sieve or muslin into clean jars. Add a fresh sprig of rosemary for decoration and again cover and store in a cool, dark place.